wild play

wild play

PARENTING ADVENTURES IN THE GREAT OUTDOORS

DAVID SOBEL

SIERRA CLUB BOOKS | SAN FRANCISCO

The Sierra Club, founded in 1892 by author and conservationist John Muir, is the oldest, largest, and most influential grassroots environmental organization in the United States. With more than a million members and supporters—and some sixty chapters across the country—we are working hard to protect our local communities, ensure an enduring legacy for America's wild places, and find smart energy solutions to stop global warming. To learn how you can participate in the Sierra Club's programs to explore, enjoy, and protect the planet, please address inquiries to Sierra Club, 85 Second Street, San Francisco, California 94105, or visit our website at www.sierraclub.org.

The Sierra Club's book publishing division, Sierra Club Books, has been a leading publisher of titles on the natural world and environmental issues for nearly half a century. We offer books to the general public as a nonprofit educational service in the hope that they may enlarge the public's understanding of the Sierra Club's concerns and priorities. The point of view expressed in each book, however, does not necessarily represent that of the Sierra Club. For more information on Sierra Club Books and a complete list of our titles and authors, please visit www.sierraclubbooks.org.

Acknowledgment of prior publication of parts of this book can be found on page 223.

Published by Sierra Club Books, 85 Second Street, San Francisco, CA 94105

Sierra Club Books are published in association with
Counterpoint (www.counterpointpress.com).

SIERRA CLUB, SIERRA CLUB BOOKS, and the Sierra Club design logos
are registered trademarks of the Sierra Club.

Book and cover design by Ingalls Design
Front cover images: top photo © Bernd Zeugswetter; middle photo © Deborah Rudy; bottom photo © iStockphoto.com/Maria Pavlova

Library of Congress Cataloging-in-Publication Data

Sobel, David, 1949–
  Wild play : parenting adventures in the great outdoors / by David Sobel.
    p. cm.
  Includes bibliographical references.
  ISBN-13: 978-1-57805-176-2 (pbk. : alk. paper)
  ISBN-10: 1-57805-176-2 (pbk. : alk. paper)
  1. Outdoor life. 2. Outdoor recreation. 3. Nature. 4. Parenting—Environmental aspects. 5. Adventure and adventurers. I. Title.
  GV191.6.S63 2011
  796.5—dc22   2010038128

Printed in the United States of America on Rolland Enviro 100 acid-free paper, which contains 100 percent post-consumer waste, processed chlorine free

Distributed by Publishers Group West
15 14 13 12 11
10 9 8 7 6 5 4 3 2 1

In memory of my friend Toby Wood

(1949–2009)

and to his sons, David and Brooks

CONTENTS

"The more slowly trees grow at first, the sounder they are at the core, and I think the same is true of human beings."

—*Henry David Thoreau*

"This connection to the earth, which is everywhere and always nurturing, is one of the greatest gifts I have ever received. It allows me to feel at home anywhere I can plant my feet in the soil and hug the trees, and it helps me find solitude and peace within myself and the world around me."

—*Tara Elliott, the author's daughter,*
in a letter to her parents

PREFACE

BEING A GOOD DAD IS HIGH ON THE LIST of the things I hope to have ac-
complished in my life. But in these postmodern times, being a good dad
isn't all that simple. There are the old chestnuts—you've got to be a good
provider, be strong, know how to fix the plumbing, show up for soccer
games and play performances, take care of cuts and scrapes. In addition,
you have to balance this yin with a little yang and perform less tangible
tasks, such as being emotionally present, knowing when to administer
Echinacea, listening for the underlying concern, and providing more love
than guidance or criticism. To this second list I add: building a bridge to
the natural world.

This book is about building that bridge. Of course, my wife, Wendy,
and I did all the other things parents try to do—help our children develop
self-respect, encourage good study habits, emphasize the virtue of being
a good friend, teach them how to stay healthy. Those endeavors will crop
up here and there. But the real focus is on bonding with the earth—that
is, creating a person–natural world relationship as an integral part of
the psyche.

One of the organizing principles of my fathering was, "I want my
children to leave for college from the same house that they were born
in." I aspired to having the local landscape mapped out on the backs of

their hands. I wanted them to grow up blueberry-stained, trail-weary, watershed-saturated, and with some apple cider—pressed from the apple trees in their backyard—flowing in their blood. Both Wendy and I had grown up in suburbia—she in California, I in Connecticut. In our own ways, we had each found fulfillment and solace in exploring the ragged edges around our neighborhoods—ravines, old fields, abandoned homes just beyond the well-tended cul-de-sacs.

My own childhood was full of experiences that marked me in this way. One was a luxurious no-school snow day on the Connecticut coast of Long Island Sound. It had dumped snow overnight—a foot and a half! I was in fifth grade. My friend Elbert, his brother, and I were intrigued by the overgrown fields, ramshackle sheds, and winding lanes behind the "haunted" house on a nearby hill. We'd made lots of forays in and around the house, but until now had not ventured into the unmapped thickety wilderness stretching from the house to the marshes of Sherwood Island State Park. What was out there? The plan was that Elbert and his brother would go into the abandoned house, exit the back door, and head into the wilderness. I'd give them a fifteen-minute lead, then follow their tracks.

A half hour later I was wallowing through almost waist-deep snow in a land far, far away: fields I'd never seen before, gulls reeling overhead. I was Lewis or Clark following the Upper Missouri, Sioux warriors lurking in the high grass. Alone, deep in the grasp of the wild world, I was aware of myself in "the exact middle of a living story," as Dylan Thomas once put it, and it was exhilarating and a little scary. I felt like part of the natural world, connected to it but also more completely myself.

Later, both Wendy and I found illumination in the mountains. As a young man I camped alone one June somewhere between Mount Jefferson and Mount Adams in the Presidential Range of New Hampshire. High above tree line, diapensia and alpine azalea were in bloom, but temperatures were in the forties, and wind-whipped fog obscured all views. The susurration of my little stove heating water for pasta kept me company, and I had the same sense of edgy fullness, of moving along in the story of my life, a living story entwined with rocky ridges and Labrador tea. These were formative experiences. As the opportunity of parenting unfolded, I knew I wanted to replicate them for my children.

Meet the Family

As this is a book designed around family stories, I'll start with some background on the setting and the players. By today's standards, we are a normal, middle-class American family. Wendy and I were married in 1985 when I was thirty-six and she was twenty-eight. The children arrived soon after. They had mostly happy childhoods. Wendy and I divorced in 2001 when Tara was fourteen and Eli was twelve. (It was very sad but also sadly normal. You'll read about it later.) We continued to be mostly conscientious parents, I hope, and my commitment to connecting our children to nature remained strong during and after the divorce. In fact, I think it's one of the things that helped us all weather the storm.

I was born in New York City in 1949. My parents divorced when I was three—I have no recollections of being together with my mother and father as a family. After this, I lived mostly in Westport, Connecticut, with my mother and her new husband, seeing my father (who eventually moved to Westport as well) every weekend. I majored in English at Williams College, graduating in 1971, then trained as an elementary school teacher, earning a master of education degree from Antioch University New England in 1973. Wet behind the ears but vastly enthusiastic, I founded and taught at the Harrisville (New Hampshire) Children's Center from 1973 to1977 and have spent most of my professional life since then engaged in teacher education at Antioch New England, including a ten-year stint as chair of the Education Department.

I try to create a healthy balance between my personal and professional lives, in large part through active outdoor, wildlands recreation. I enjoy the thrill of cold water, so I try to swim outdoors at least three-fourths of the year, from March to November. I have learned the hills, lost roads, and hidden marshes of New Hampshire's Monadnock region through exploratory cross-country skiing, skating, and mountain biking.

I indulge in downhill skiing despite its impacts on the environment. And I enjoy the craft of making apple cider.

Wendy's mom was from Costa Rica and her father from upstate New York. Born in 1957, she grew up in Los Angeles until her family suffered a double tragedy: her father died after being hit by a car while crossing the street, and her mother succumbed to cancer a few years later. Wendy moved to the San Francisco Bay Area and lived with her uncle and aunt's large family. After a year of college in Hawaii, she graduated from the University of California–San Diego with a bachelor's degree in psychology. We met when she was studying dance therapy at Antioch University New England; she completed her master's degree and eventually earned another degree in organization and management. She has spent her professional life as a high school and college counselor, dean of student affairs, college instructor, and private-practice psychologist. She now lives in Keene, New Hampshire. Her recreational interests include running, lots of dance, fine cooking, regular travel to warm places, keeping her Spanish tuned up, and cultivating close friendships.

Tara was born on a spectacularly blue-scarlet-pumpkin day in early October 1986 at home in Harrisville. She grew up and went away to college from the same house (mostly), graduating from Bennington College in 2009 as a theatre and dance major. Tara has had wanderlust from an early age, and we've supported her in working with Russian orphans, doing *commedia dell'arte* street theatre in Italy, and spending the last half of her senior year in high school on a teaching internship in Costa Rica. She also did a college semester abroad in Chile, studying education and social policy and perfecting her Spanish. Starting in childhood, she directed and acted in a wide array of theatre and dance productions and has worked as a gardener, landscaper, and waitress. She has been the drama teacher at the Vinalhaven School, a K–12 public school on Vinalhaven, one of Maine's fifteen offshore communities.

Eli was born in a blizzard in February 1989. The first couple of weeks, even the first couple of years, were tough sledding for him healthwise, but he is now a strapping lad. Like Tara, he grew up and went away to college from the same house (mostly). He is currently a student in the Rubenstein School of Natural Resources at the University of Vermont. During his sophomore year, he did a semester abroad studying sustainable development in Belize. His February birth imprinted on his soul, and he is a child of winter: a competitive freestyle skier and winner of many slope-style ski competitions. He's also enthusiastic about finding cool swimming holes, whitewater kayaking, *salsa caliente,* jazz piano, and urban rails. He has worked as a videographer, painter, carpenter, and camp counselor.

Until Tara and Eli entered middle school, Wendy worked as a private-practice psychologist and college instructor about half-time; after that, she worked full-time. Although I was a full-time college faculty member, I always stayed home on Tuesdays to do childcare or take the children out of school for adventures or pick them up after school. Parenting responsibilities were shared pretty evenly. We ate dinners together as a family almost always until the divorce. No doubt an important fact of the children's upbringing is that we didn't have television for the first six years or so after Tara was born, and after that we had only a video player. When I got Direct TV in 2009 it was the end of a long era of minimal television.

Instead, we prioritized being outside with our children. We played in the backyard, gardened, rambled to the gorge, hiked Monadnock and lots of other local summits, swam every possible day, bicycled. We also made a big point of taking family vacations. This is where we spent much of our disposable income. When the children were young, we took them out of school for two weeks each May to go to Cape Cod, spent a week each summer on an island off the coast of Maine, and escaped to islands in the Caribbean each winter for a week or two. Tara, Eli, and I skied at least one day a week during the winter. The natural world was as important a learning environment as school.

Our Local Landscape

About a year before Tara was born, Wendy and I bought a 1789 Cape in Harrisville. It was definitely a fixer-upper. The day we moved in, the roof came off in the first of seven major renovations we did on the house.

We chose it because it was on a quiet road with about ten houses, all part of an old village center. It had a great backyard with five overgrown but still-bearing apple trees. Bill and Irene, surrogate grandparents, lived next door. There was easy access to semi-wilderness out the back door, yet it was only a twenty-minute drive on good roads to Keene, where we worked.

The walk to the gorge went like this: Walk through the woodshed out the back door. Pass through the yard, under the apple trees and past the garden, and hitch a left into Bill and Irene's field. At the end of the field, cross over the stone wall and descend a couple hundred yards to the trail along the gorge. Straight ahead through the woods is the stream coming out of the gorge into Russell Reservoir. Turn left on the trail winding upstream toward the dam. As you enter into a hemlock grove, the stream gets close to the trail on the right. If you follow the little side trail Eli built when he was about eleven, you can walk along the cliff top, peer-ing down about fifty feet into the waterfall and pool, the tannin-stained stream snaking along the gorge bottom. Cross the Monadnock-Sunapee trail and arrive at the dam, about twenty-five feet high, that holds back Howe Reservoir. There's a little grassy area here and the water is deep. It was our private family skinny-dipping spot.

Since loops are more interesting than walking back the same way you came, we'd take a different route home: Follow the trail out to the road, over a little ridge. Turn left up Brown Road to get to our house. It was our own little bit of wildness.

As the kids grew, their significant natural world expanded outward— a natural process that is also a central principle of this book. First just our yard, then the nearby neighbors. Then down the road to the school in one direction, and the Four Corners in the other direction—about half a mile either way. Each year on her birthday, from when Tara was about five till she was fifteen, I constructed a treasure hunt that was suitable to her current stage of development. At five, it was just in the yard, at seven it stretched to the neighbor's house. By age ten, the cake was hidden in a pipe at the base of the Howe Reservoir Dam about three-quarters of a mile away. The children had to follow clues to get there by themselves. (Eli often went along, but we had different birthday traditions for him.)

Harrisville and the surrounding Monadnock Highlands region are chock-full of lakes. In a similar outward-expanding way, we took advantage of them for swimming, skating, canoeing, and camping. We felt blessed that there were a half dozen great places to swim within a ten-minute drive of the house. When Tara and Eli were in middle childhood, the town beach at Harrisville Pond was a regular hangout. And Harrisville itself, a preserved but lived-in nineteenth-century textile mill village, was the Norman Rockwell small-town America that most parents dream about. Our children grew up in a fortunate landscape and community.

I'VE WRITTEN SEVERAL OTHER BOOKS in my professional field—childhood development with an emphasis on children interacting with nature—that are directed mainly at teachers, environmental educators, and academics. I occasionally brought my personal experiences of parenting into these books, but by their nature they stayed in the background.

However, I've been as deeply engaged in my fatherhood as in my professional life, and I had conscious aims in parenting that dovetailed with my work. (There's nothing like actual parenting to make theories look foolish, and it kept my work grounded.) Although I have published some essays that centered on my outdoor adventures with Tara and Eli, there was much more untapped material in my journals. And recently, as my children have passed milestones in young adulthood, I've felt more and more compelled to sum up our two decades of history as father and daughter and son engaged in purposeful, joyful exploration of the natural world.

So this is first and foremost a memoir of that history, with parents as its primary audience. What I've learned on this adventure is useful, I hope, for parents as well as educators. I write here as a parent (albeit one with special training) for other parents who desire, as I did and do, that their children grow up with dirt under their fingernails, glints of sunlight in their eyes, and a deep sense of hope about life on earth.

Like any memoir, this one is the particular history of a particular set of people—a family with extensive and privileged access to a four-season life in the outdoors and a strong urge to maximize that access. Not every family is so lucky or so strongly inclined. Yet I believe that virtually any family with a will to expand their children's horizons in ways that can happen only in nature can find their own ways there, perhaps inspired by these examples.

INTRODUCTION
Trails into the Woods

"I WON'T GROW UP. I don't want to go to school!" my daughter declares. My throat constricts, and tears rise. But they're not tears of frustration, they're tears of happiness. In this snapshot from a decade ago, Tara is eleven and is onstage playing her first leading role in a summer production of *Peter Pan*. It has all come together for her. Her movement is fluid, her diction is clear, and even her singing voice is assured and strong.

But the tears are more than just the signature of a proud parent. Bruno Bettelheim contends that many children choose one story from childhood that becomes their raison d'etre, the source of meaning throughout life. *Peter Pan* was the central compelling story of my own childhood. I had sharp images of the lost world—lagoons, tropical beaches with crystal-clear water, the underground house, the eerie woods. When I skittered from tree to tree in the Connecticut woods, I could hear the "Yo ho, yo ho!" of pirates echoing in the foggy thickets.

Flopped on the living room couch, I memorized the lyrics to all the songs from the 1950s musical production filmed for television: "Tender Shepherd," "I've Gotta Crow," and of course Tiger Lily's "Ugg-a-wugg, ugg-a-wugg, ugg-a-ugg, ugg-a-wugg wa!" I couldn't have explained why it meant so much to me; I don't think I really understood it myself. Maybe it was a bit of anticipatory nostalgia—the knowledge that I was at the end of childhood and in a few years I'd be looking back with a sense of loss and yearning. Or maybe I was getting the first apprehension of a personal theme, or what Carl Jung describes as the question each individual brings to the world.

The character of Peter Pan and issues of growing up got woven into the fabric of my parenting life. I came to appreciate that growing up slowly was valuable for children. I recognized that the "lost world" of Peter Pan and Captain Hook represented the imaginative fantasy worlds children often enter into during free play in the outdoors. Using this as a model, I created similar story worlds for our family that drew on the local natural worlds our children were immersed in.

When Eli was born, he almost died from a severe staph infection in the first few days of his life. Wendy and I sang "Tender Shepherd" as we rested our hands on him amid the tangle of wires and tubes providing life support. We just wanted him to have a chance to grow up, to know the exhilarating beauty of this world. We willed it with a purity of heart. During their early childhood years, I sang the children to sleep most nights. "Distant Melody," another *Peter Pan* lullaby, was part of the bedtime ritual. And though we never quite got around to reading the James Barrie original, the kids always played at flying, and I was often Captain Hook.

So, Tara, on the verge of puberty at age eleven, is playing Peter and I feel a confusion of happiness and sadness. Happy because she's got presence, she projects, and she loves pouring herself into the role. Happy because the whole production is a wonderful combination of adolescents and younger children, silliness and commitment, work and play. Sad because Tara's childhood is in its twilight, and while I look forward to the woman she is becoming, I will miss the girl she's been.

Losing Our Way

I also felt, in that snapshot from the late 1990s, a sense of completion in knowing that my children's growing up had been relatively charmed and full. We lived in a safe neighborhood with room to roam. As a family, we had the resources and commitment to prioritize family vacations, sit-down dinners, and outdoor play. One evening that spring, for instance, I succumbed to nine-year-old Eli's badgering to take him swimming. It was dark and drizzly but surprisingly warm for May in New Hampshire. At the tiny beach on Russell Reservoir down the road, we relished the warm night air, devoid of the mind-boggling blackflies that finally disappear at dusk. Transcending their bickering, Tara and Eli gallivanted into the water, whooping and laughing. We bobbed in the shallow water, specu-lating that we were probably the only people in the whole Monadnock region crazy enough to go swimming that night. Our family culture of play brought us together after a day on separate paths.

But many families aren't as fortunate, and even ours fell prey to a per-vasive kind of timesickness—the feeling that there's never enough time. "Get your shoes on, Eli, or we'll be late for school!" Or, "I'd love to play checkers with you, Tara, but it'll have to wait till tomorrow." And tomorrow comes and goes without any double jumps. It seems that we suffer from a temporal case of our eyes being bigger than our stomachs. There's soccer and shopping and swim lessons and homework. We have to fit in orthodontist appointments, picking up grandmother's prescrip-tion, and teacher-parent meetings.

A study some time ago found that people have a tendency to spend about 10 percent more than their income. It doesn't matter whether you make $20,000 or $200,000 a year, there just never seems to be enough to pay the bills. I'd guess that, similarly, most of us commit to more than our time budget allows, so there's never enough time to squeeze in all the things we've said yes to. What's getting lost in the rush?

Childhood is, I think, and especially children's connection with na-ture. And timesickness isn't the only culprit. A virus of dread and inse-curity has crept into the hearts of many parents in urban and suburban America. In her article "Childhood Lost," Melissa Fay Greene reminisces about "the deliciously idle, random hours between 3:30 and 6:00" of her childhood, when she used to ramble the neighborhood, walking her dog, having buckeye wars, playing Witch Hazel. She bemoans the fact that her children have no such inclinations, and that she subliminally discourages them, reflecting,

> I want to stand in the front yard and sing out their lovely names at dusk and have them suddenly appear in the damp yard around me like little fireflies. But I can't. I can't let them roam. I don't have my mother's confidence that the world is a safe place. . . . Something irreplaceable has been lost. A certain sense of freedom, of fun, has gone out of the world. The golden age of childhood is gone.

It's the Bogeyman Syndrome—fear exaggerated beyond the scope of real threat. (This concept was originally articulated by Richard Louv in *Childhood's Future* and elaborated more recently in *Last Child in the Woods*.) Please understand that I am as horrified as you by shooting events in schools, unexplainable examples of youth violence, and childhood abductions. But few of these dangers come anywhere close to threatening the lives of our children as much as riding in a car, something they do every day.

The Bogeyman Syndrome is in great part a result of the rampant media-ization of our lives. We are disproportionately deluged with examples of tragedies and violence. As a result, our perception of danger is much greater than the actual risk. For example, sociologist Joel Best reviewed seventy-six stories of Halloween sadism from 1958 to 1984: tales of razor blades in apples, drugs baked into cookies, and so on, but found not one case in which a child was seriously harmed. The vast majority of these "reports" turned out to be examples of urban folklore.

Concurrent with such rising fears has been the rise of electronic entertainment in the form of television, video games, and computer recreation, which lure children away from stickball, jump rope, and capture the flag, and invite them into finger-tapping shoot-'em-up games. Still more recent and revolutionary has been the co-opting of children's social life by texting and screen-based social networking. In one sense it's the same problem we've always faced with TV, only now the screens have proliferated. The world has become vastly more plugged in even since my children were growing up, and it's a real challenge for families. Neither I or anyone else has a comprehensive answer, but certainly it has to start with parents both setting limits and providing alternatives that engage children deeply. And they must start early on both fronts: controlling the amount of screen time kids are allowed—whether with TV, computers, gaming devices, or mobile phones—in early to middle childhood. And making sure that the alternative magic of the natural world has enough chances to work on them and take hold during those early years.

Other factors contribute to the trend of lost time outdoors: More and more families have two working parents, so children have to be in child-care programs, where supervisors must be vigilant about insurance liability. Schools want kids to read earlier, do more homework, and start algebra in seventh grade. Organized sports start kids younger and younger, and year-round soccer gobbles up any spare time children might have to take the dog for a walk in the woods or build a hideout behind the garage.

As we hang out on couches, bathed in PlayStation glare, the memory of kick-the-can, the rules for jacks, the joy of climbing trees fade from consciousness. Parents forget that they once did these things, children never learn, and insurance advisers convince us that it's unsafe to let our children's friends do these things when they're at our homes. Nature becomes a museum exhibit, something to be seen and not touched. We've lost our way.

These trends have been widely chronicled and lamented, so I don't need to discuss them further here. Suffice to say that, just as native plants are endangered and traditional cultures become globalized, a childhood of outdoor play is fading away. Outdoor play is like the forest that gets cut down lot by lot for the new housing development. Each new home is only a small incursion. It's hard to object to just one more house, but bit by bit, the roamable woods transmute to Kentucky bluegrass.

The magic and mystery of the deep forest, with its fantastical inhabitants, was once part of actual childhood experience, but more and more it's relegated to storybooks or is experienced online. Think of Tinker Bell after she drinks the poison intended for Peter. Her twinkle dims, her bell loses its lilt. Do we still believe in fairies? Well, I'll stick my neck out and say, yes, I believe in fairies and stories and certain kinds of magic, in treasure hunts and secret paths into the woods.

Prioritizing Outdoor Play

Childhood needs to be spacious enough for outdoor play to take on a prominent role. And not just because such play is fun but because it's biologically adaptive. Just as bobcat kittens play to develop the necessary physical dexterity for hunting, children play to develop their mental dexterity. Play helps children understand that the world is malleable, that their actions on the world can make a difference. A board isn't just a board, it's a plank to walk; it's access to the first branch of the tree; it's a jump for horses. Playing with natural materials in childhood prepares us for playing with ideas behind a desk. Playing multiple roles in a school dramatic production prepares us for the multiple roles of being a leader, a follower, a peacemaker, or a midwife's assistant in our adult lives. Our parenting challenge is to resist the tide of overprotectionism and provide opportunities for children to create their own play realities in backyards, neighborhoods, and urban green spaces.

In my own parenting, I have consciously sought to create and cultivate diverse forms of natural play with and for Tara and Eli. My consistent hope was that this would both foster mental dexterity and social adeptness, and forge an immutable bond between them and the natural world. Paul Shepard, in *The Tender Carnivore and the Sacred Game,* describes the power of childhood experiences this way:

> It's no accident, nor is it the design of any particular culture, that ten is the golden age of childhood. It is at this time that all the child has worked for seems to come to fruition. He is an expert in play, in factual knowledge and the concrete. . . . Ten years is that landmark of the lost idyll, the subject of future nostalgia. The ten-year-old's euphoria will imprint on his surroundings, drawing him back in adult years to the scenes of childhood.

If the child has enough euphoric outdoor experiences in childhood—experiences in which she feels merged, continuous, at one with the hedge she's hidden in, the baby bird in her hands, the darkened pond—then her affinity for the natural world will never go away. And that affinity will become the soil in which an environmental ethic takes root.

One morning after dropping off Tara at high school, I took time for a walk around the pond on the school's nature trail. The signposts were faded and tilting; beaver-felled birches crisscrossed the path. A barberry thicket had run rampant and completely obliterated most signs of a beaten path. Yet old bridges remained, and there were just enough clues left to make out the original intent. The trail was obscured but not completely forgotten.

That's where we are now. We've still got the chance to give our children the life-shaping benefits of outdoor play. Before the tidal wave of electrons crashes on shore and obliterates all signs of biological life, let's clear out the trails into the meadows and woods, unearth the vestiges of our natural play instincts, and brush off the accumulated dust.

A Developmental Framework

Think of the complex trail network at a community nature center. Starting at the signboard in the parking lot, the path at first runs through cultivated grounds, across a meadow, around a small pond. In the near distance, trails wander off into the forest—rocky glens, a birch grove, foothills and dales. After some serious walking, more trails lead you up onto ledges and past caves, to the rocky ridge overlooking the meadow and woods below. There are many ways of moving through the landscape, but all paths eventually lead up and away.

Similarly, the landscape of childhood contains varied habitats, or stages of development. My training, teaching, and parenting have all taught me that at each stage we are designed to seek something different in our relationship with the outside world. What we find in the meadow of early childhood is different from what we search for in the forest of the elementary years. And completely new views are revealed from the rocky outcrops of adolescence. As parents, educators, and community leaders, we serve our children best by being aware of the lay of the land in the child-nature landscape and providing the most fitting kinds of challenges and opportunities at different stages.

When I was learning to be a teacher, one of my psychology professors noted, "When children come to first grade, they can do two things really well. They can run around and they can talk. And one of the first things we say to them is, 'Sit down and be quiet.' Right away, we take away exactly the things they know how to do." Good education and good parenting do just the opposite: the core idea is to focus on building strengths rather than remediating weaknesses. This is at odds with the dominant paradigm operating in many public schools, where the assumption is that we have to make all children equally good at all things. Children come to school and life with different passions and gifts—some can talk a blue streak, some easily feel at one with nature, some don't mind getting muddy, some are fascinated by bugs—and our goal should be to sense and guide these passions.

At each stage in development, new opportunities unfold in the interplay between child and nature: the child asks a series of questions, and the natural world provides a progression of answers. This interplay needs to be mediated by parents to maximize the likelihood that the right answers are discovered. It's like the birthday treasure hunts I used to design for Tara. At age five, children follow their string through the confines of the yard, winding it up on a stick, so they are assured of finding the treasure. At ten, the clues are tricky and the children have to search far and wide throughout the neighborhood to succeed. The thoughtful parent calibrates the challenge to the developmental sophistication of the child. The parent of the five-year-old ensures safety; the parent of the ten-year-old encourages problem solving and navigation. The five-year-old unwraps a gift of wonder; the ten-year-old unwraps a gift of exploration.

Henry David Thoreau said, "The more slowly trees grow at first, the sounder they are at the core, and I think the same is true of human beings." One of my underlying assumptions, the principle on which all my ideas about childhood development and nature rest, is the notion that evolution has designed human beings with a long childhood for a reason. The simple explanation is that childhood gives us the opportunity to develop faculties and skills that will be crucial to our becoming effective, contributing members of an adult community—and of a healthy ecosystem. Shorten childhood, and you sacrifice the potential for creating whole people and a healthy natural world. I am suggesting that, from a natural-selection perspective, a long childhood is adaptive: the human species has evolved a long childhood in order to provide an extended series of learning opportunities. The longer the child remains flexible and open, the more he can be shaped by culture and the natural world. The challenge now is to shift those forces into better balance.

A developmental perspective also underlies this book's structure. Each of the three parts contains a set of chapters introduced by a "prelude," or framing discussion of developmental issues around the stages of early childhood, middle childhood, and adolescence. In these preludes I use landscape metaphors to introduce and describe aspects of each developmental stage and the kind of parent-child-nature relationships we want to cultivate.

This is part of a conscious strategy on my part to replace mechanistic metaphors with organic metaphors. If we consistently analogize the mind to the computer, the person to the machine, we develop a hidden paradigm of assuming that the technological world is the source of reality. If instead we use metaphors that emerge from natural history and ecological systems, we acknowledge the true evolutionary sources of our thinking. For instance, some neurophysiologists now contend that it's much more appropriate to analogize the neural networking in the brain to a jungle than to a computer.

In Part One, which deals with early childhood (age two to six or seven), the metaphor is exploring the meadow. The meadow is sunlit, bright, close to home, full of a profusion of activity and chatter. Large trees provide islands of shade. There's a small pond. Birds sing, small mammals gallivant. Parents and children play together in close proximity. Dads tell stories in the shade. Moms sing songs. Children make believe they are bunnies. Families explore nature together.

In Part Two, covering middle childhood (age six or seven to twelve or thirteen), I focus on exploring the forest beyond the meadow. There are glades of hardwoods, birches for bending, big spreading beeches to climb, patches of raspberries and blackberries. The land drops off into hemlock woods and down to a stream where you can balance-walk tree trunks to the other side. Sometimes parents and children are here together, collecting berries or swimming in a pool in the stream. Other times children follow secret paths to hidden forts, with their friends or on their own.

Part Three moves on to adolescence (age thirteen or fourteen to young adulthood), where the focus shifts to exploring pathways that ascend from the forest up to the rocky ridge. There are boulder caves for secret ceremonies, steep slopes for risky adventures on rock or snow. Sometimes parents belay their children as they climb on their own. Other times, mom and dad wish them well and watch nervously as their children head off into the wilderness beyond the ridge.

The chapters that form each part are chiefly accounts of my experiences outdoors with Tara and Eli over the course of their young lives, from toddlerhood to their twenties. Many of the chapters started out as essays written around the time of the events they recount, which then were revised as this book was assembled.

The stories and reflections in the essays were set down in the moment, while I was a father of children who were then at the age depicted. So my perspective is from that time and place, and events are sometimes told in the present tense—for example, in a reproduced journal entry or a scrap of dialogue. "A Little Love between Us and the Trees" captures my thinking about parenting in nature when Tara was four, and "Bare Hands and Bear Dens" when she was nine. "Assessing Ice" finds her on the verge of adolescence at thirteen, and "The Door in the Rock" was written when she was eighteen. Similarly, you'll follow the growing up of my son, Eli, and the evolution of my thinking through "Deer Inside" (Eli at about age two through four), "Burning Brush" (Eli at nine), "Doing Tuckerman's" (Eli at thirteen), and "Bow Loop and Brimstone" (Eli at nineteen).

The narrative ingredients of each chapter include in-the-moment conversations, journal entries, writings by Tara and Eli, and my later recollections of family history—plus some supporting quotations from other observers. You'll quickly discover that, in addition to direct contact with nature, I pay much attention to the mediation of experience through storytelling, which played a huge role in my own parenting. I frequently made up stories and encouraged Tara and Eli to exercise their storytelling muscles as well.

Looking back over the result, it strikes me that I didn't really understand the developmental issues at work or the appropriate ways for children to engage with nature until I was inside each stage, working out the relationships among my children, the natural world, and myself. And the writing process itself helped me understand what I experienced and what I believe. "Assessing Ice" found me struggling to come to terms with the end of Tara's childhood. "Moving in My Heart" was a cathartic attempt to process the pain of divorce and the loss of family life through recounting a period of immersion in the natural world.

Journals and Parenting

A few days before Tara was born, I bought a new journal with the intent of documenting this new phase of my life, and the beginnings of hers. I wanted to track my own emerging sense of fatherhood—the emotional roller coaster, the ways in which being a father would change me. Moreover, in the spirit of some of the great developmental psychologists, I hoped the journal would help me capture my new daughter's unique language and ways of being. Just as using a camera can help one to focus more closely, I hoped the journal would help me to listen more closely and to capture fleeting observations and reflections.

Remembering conversations with children is like remembering dreams—if you don't write them down right away, they're gone in the wink of an eye. Without having written them down, I never would have seen the patterns and relationships that emerged over months and years. I was fascinated, returning to my journals after a few years, to see connections between conversations that had completely disappeared from my conscious memory.

The process of keeping a journal about my children helped me to be a better parent and allowed me to think about how I wanted to cultivate their biological inclinations toward nature. I'd been a conscientious journal keeper already, but my focus had been on dreams, adventures, and exotic travels. Now my attention turned to observations of Tara's, and later Eli's, behavior and language. But the journal also became a vehicle for exploring the meaning of fatherhood and how parenthood enlarged my emotional world. Although I had taught human development for years prior to becoming a parent, I wasn't prepared for the waves of startling new feelings that washed over me in those first few years—feelings of protectiveness, anger, and frustration; joy unlike anything I'd ever experienced before Tara came along; the long sleepless nights of worry about Eli's health.

Illustrating my academic bent, much of what I documented was how the children's language developed, and our spontaneous conversations at dinnertime or bedtime about big issues. As often as possible, I tried to transcribe Tara and Eli's comments and our conversations soon after they occurred. Sometimes, in the midst of a particularly good description, I'd jump up, run to get my journal, and transcribe verbatim what they were saying. They got used to this slightly awkward process and accepted it.

Being a conscientious journaler is one of the best things I did as a parent. It helped me to listen better and to anticipate when interesting things were about to be said, and it provided a record of experiences and conversations that otherwise would have been lost. As an unanticipated bonus, it modeled the virtue of journal keeping and encouraged both Tara and Eli (to a lesser extent) to become journalers.

More to the point, this book would not have been possible without my journals. The illustrative details, the salient quotations, and the patterns of understanding would have all evaporated if this material hadn't been preserved on the spot. In some ways, I treated parenting as if I were an ethnographer trying to describe a new culture—though, admittedly, I sometimes selected comments that illustrated things I wanted to write about.

As the children got older, I collected pieces of their writing from school. Tara became a journal keeper early on and sometimes let me read what she wrote. On occasion, when I knew I was writing something for publication, I'd ask one or the other to write their recollections of certain shared events. This is the source of the quoted material in "Assessing Ice" and "Doing Tuckerman's," for instance. I have corrected grammar and spelling in their writing but have tried to preserve the gist intact. At other times I have reconstructed their comments from conversations; when I felt they were old enough, I let them read my transcripts and invited them to correct anything that didn't sound like their words.

For many of the reasons just noted, I strongly advocate that parents keep a journal of observations about their children. Regardless of whether you use it for any other purpose, journaling enables you to record the real, complex, often confusing welter of experiences and emotions involved in child rearing and make sense of them after the fact, rather than relying on the distortions and generalizations of memory alone. The rich layering of detail that can be preserved in a journal is closer to life as it is lived than even the clearest memory—and, not coincidentally, analogous to the richness of the natural world as I experienced it with Tara and Eli.

In fact, I could say that this book came to be largely because of my journals. My hope is that the result will spark some ideas for explorations and adventures with your children, experiences that will transmute into foundational stories for them. Think of this as a kind of trail guide, a series of guided walks through a wild landscape, with each set of chapters helping you find your way to places you've never been before. There are plenty of ways to get where you and your children want to go—no one best path, but lots of cool places to discover.

PART ONE

early childhood
in the meadow

PRELUDE

PARENTING CHILDREN INTO NATURE in early childhood should be like an afternoon in a meadow. Here, parents and children together explore the nearby natural world—the backyard, the playground, the fountain, the urban cemetery, the alleyway, the farmers' market. Even before this, though, in a child's first two years, groundwork is being laid for her relationship with the world around her. So I'll start there.

Watch a mother and infant at the beach, snuggled together on a blanket. The infant notices a whelk shell, crawls over to it, looks back at mom as if to ask, "Is it okay to pick this up?" Mom smiles, confirming assent. The child grabs it, looks inside, shakes it, smells it, and tosses it toward a piece of driftwood. A wave hits the shore with a large *thwack!* that startles the infant. He hustles back to his mother's reassuring arms.

In infancy, the child creates a basic trusting relationship with mom and dad and then, in tiny, incremental incidents like this one on the beach, comes to understand that exploring, touching, and smelling new things is okay.

One of the challenges parents face during infancy is how to resist the cultural emphasis on fostering individuation quickly—in plain language, the pressure to encourage kids to grow up fast. There are compelling reasons to prolong childhood, and parents who understand this believe in letting nature take its time. Some mothers choose to nurse their children until they are two or three years old, well beyond the normal six months to one year. They get criticized for indulging their children, perhaps stunting their development. But many other cultures support breastfeeding for several years, and many mothers feel that a long breastfeeding experience serves to create a deeper bond.

Another message that can be counterproductive is our modern obsession with cleanliness. Cultural anthropologist Paul Shepard contends that the infant's tendency to stick things in her mouth may have adaptive value. As the infant sucks on sticks, grass, dirt, and other natural objects, her intestinal system is taking in the bacterial fauna of the local environment and developing natural immunities to those fauna. This interpenetration between the child's body and the natural world is fostered as long as we don't get all flustered when children put things in their mouths. We should support (obviously with some intervention) rather than deny their natural inclinations.

Parents may also choose to sustain very early childhood by providing a family bed experience. Some parents choose to have their child in the same bed or the same room for many years, believing that there's no need to force a young child into the isolation of sleeping alone early on. In our family, though Tara and Eli graduated from the family bed experience fairly early, Wendy and I maintained a tradition of lying down at night with them as they were going to sleep. We did it with Tara until she was about ten and with Eli into early adolescence. Not only did it provide a sense of physical security, but it also offered an opportunity for marvelous conversations. For many years I sang or told stories, but later my son wanted to chat about the birth of the universe or how airplanes work or the problem he had with a friend at school. In Japan and India this practice of lying down with children at bedtime is still very common.

Both extended nursing and the family bed experience in early childhood provide a deepened sense of security, a sense that the child is held within the protective matrix of the family. Individuation is necessary, but it doesn't need to happen so fast. Bonding within a safe family is a precursor to bonding with the earth. If the child feels that relationships with parents and other caregivers are safe, she'll more likely be willing to move out into the explorable world.

Early childhood, starting around age two, is a time for fostering empathy, for encouraging children's sense of connectedness with the animals, trees, rocks, soil, and water of the nearby world—for exploring the meadow. When our children were small, we twitched our noses like bunnies, soared like swallows, swam like seals, and made temporary aquaria for crayfish so we could play with them and then let them go. I wanted them to feel life from the inside out, to know what it felt like to be inside a raccoon's skin as it tried to take the top off the garbage can. Identifying with animals by "becoming" them precedes saving them.

This is also the most intense period of childhood for language development, metaphor making, and fantasy, and it is crucially important that children develop these faculties during this phase. Some neurophysiologists contend that early childhood is the key period of development of the brain's right hemisphere—the visual, spatial, metaphoric hemisphere—which is balanced later as the more sequential and logical left hemisphere develops and elaborates in middle childhood. In any case, it is now clear that there is a biologically programmed phase of language development from birth until about six years old. Thus it's our responsibility to provide a language-rich environment during this period and build on the rich metaphor-making capacities children have, especially between two and six years old.

The natural world provides a wealth of raw materials to foster this growth. Using nature as a primary source, parents should read animal stories to their children, encourage descriptive language, imitate animal sounds, tell stories based on everyday occurrences, be attentive to children's descriptions, and use their invented words as part of explanations.

Nature-based language and stories should be generously woven into the fabric of early childhood life. It doesn't need to dominate—lots of conversation will center on food, friends, household rules, and health—but it should be a persistent presence.

If you listen closely, you'll discover that children freely use metaphor, natural and otherwise, at this early age. A child will take a bite out of a piece of toast, notice the resulting shape, and say, "It's the moon," or he'll look at the back of a chair and see a ladder. This ability to make metaphors, see analogies between the shape of your hand and the shape of a fish, is the kind of thing that's tested later in life on the Miller Analogies Test and is also an attribute of adult creative thinkers.

Playing with language at this stage helps children develop mental flexibility later in life. If we can be responsive to children's organic metaphors and use them in our explanations, we're demonstrating that the natural world shapes how we talk and how we think: "Your shoes are lined up just the way the swallows sit on the telephone wire." We thus model interdependence and interpenetration in daily conversation. Similarly, some families preserve the charming mispronunciations of common words by young children. When I was growing up, we always talked about having "pisgetty" for dinner because that's the way my sister said "spaghetti." One metaphor that emerged from a conversation with three-year-old Tara was the "water ring," a way of understanding the water cycle, which expanded to become a starting point to explain the cycle of life and the idea of reincarnation.

The chapters that follow look at various ways in which our family explored the meadows of early childhood—through being outdoors and through telling stories that offered comfort while building bonds with the natural world.

In "A Little Love between Us and the Trees," you'll see Tara and me working on the cultivation and preservation of metaphor in early language. From describing the color of sounds, to conversations about what trees eat, to analogizing the water cycle and the great wheel of life, talking about nature with children makes nature a part of their mental structures, and being attentive to what they say can open parents' eyes and ears in remarkable ways.

"Deer Inside" describes a dream Eli had when he was around three years old, and then a set of stories that emerged from that dream. Here I advocate for family storytelling that creates friendly relationships between children and animals that live nearby.

"Moon-Jumping Nights" looks at how children personify the natural world. Tara empathizes with dead fish, talks to the moon, and develops relationships with fairies. (Now in her early twenties, she recently recalled learning to ride a bike at age six; the breakthrough was when Wendy, before letting go of the bike, told her that the fairies would be flying alongside supporting her. Believing in the fairies' assistance gave Tara the oomph she needed to pedal and balance on her own.)

"Deer Inside" introduces the idea of magical realism as a family art, and "The Mermaids and the Necklace" takes it further, with stories set in various locales during a lakeside vacation. Cultivating such imaginative worlds in nature during childhood can nurture an ability to access wonder and delight that persists into adult life.

"Together in Dreamland" describes the children's first experience of being separated from their mother, at ages four and two. Here I experiment with a simple form of lucid dreaming, using archetypal nature imagery to help Tara cope with sadness and feel closer to her absent mom.

As firm categories and concrete thinking emerge in middle childhood, metaphoric and magical thinking takes a backseat for a while, hopefully to emerge again in adolescence. If we nourish it in early childhood, give it form and substance, it stays quietly alive, ready for action—like the oyster reef that protects the shoreline during big storms. The young child is a creature of the meadow, and the meadow lives inside him. Some of his words are rooted in meadow soil, he plays with grasshoppers and rabbits, he eats food that comes from the meadow. When he grows up, leaving that safe, protected world of childhood behind, and perhaps works in an office, he will hold on to the deep memory of the meadow within.

A Little Love between Us and the Trees
Language and Metaphor in Tara's World

While Tara was an infant, my developmental journal contained mostly reflections on how parenting was changing me and ideas for how to be a good dad of an infant. But as she entered toddlerhood and began to talk more volubly, my record become more and more focused on how her language was developing, the way it ranged freely through metaphor, and especially how she described what she perceived in her physical world. I was particularly fascinated with the language that emerged during our adventures or play outdoors—at the beach, riding sheep at a farm, on night walks.

While most adults experience the senses as distinct and separate, like the separate rooms in a traditional house, children can experience them as being fluidly merged, like the kitchen, dining room, and living room in an architecturally modern house with only partial walls delineating the spaces. Experiences don't fit into neat sensory-mode packages; seeing a beautiful meadow can easily evoke musical sounds for children, or it might taste delicious to them.

Let me share an assortment of examples from Tara's speech in her second and third years to illustrate how this metaphoric way of seeing is deeply ensconced in the child's perception of the world. The first two examples are visual analogies, in which Tara describes how one thing looks in terms of another thing.

AUGUST 23, 1988 (AGE 1 YEAR, 10 MONTHS)   A beach game played two or three times this summer has been "playing gator." Tara and Toby (an adult friend) try to hide behind the rocks in shallow water. I am the alligator and creep through the water, with just the top of my head sticking out, searching for them. When I get close, I lunge and roar and miss them. They scream and laugh and splash. The last time we played this was about six weeks ago.

On a long afternoon walk down to the Otter Pond, Tara and I stop by the edge of the water to look. I point out a frog sitting still in the water, its head slightly above the water and its body floating below the surface. Tara whispers to me, "Frog playing gator," making the analogy between the posture of my body during the playing of the game and the frog's posture.

NOVEMBER 26, 1988 (2Y, 2M)   On a walk today, we stop to watch a bunch of midges circling in a cluster in the air. Tara says, "They're juggling," referring to the clowns we saw about a week ago. We had said very little about juggling since the circus and it had not seemed to have much impact that day, but now I realize that the haze of midges does look similar to the balls suspended in the air in front of a juggler.

Keep in mind that Tara is only two years old here, yet she's clearly storing images in her mind, often extracted from the natural world, connecting words with them, and then reapplying them in very different situations. This is an early form of the process of insight, of making connections between one situation and another. It's the foundation of the problem-solving tactics we try to cultivate as parents and teachers. And here it was emerging naturally.

The Metaphoric Roots of Early Language

To help understand the intriguing aspects of Tara's early language, I turned to Heinz Werner, a German developmental psychologist writing in the early twentieth century. Werner was fascinated by children's tendency to experience the world synesthetically, in blended sensory modes. In other words, the senses of seeing, hearing, smelling, tasting, and touching often merge together in a child's perception. Adults are familiar with this in our experience of smell and taste. Things that smell bad evoke a bad taste in our mouth. Likewise, when we can't smell, it's difficult to taste. But young children sometimes experience such blending in seeing and hearing as well. One specific form of synesthesia is called chromesthesia, or "color hearing." Individuals who experience chromesthesia experience certain sounds as having specific colors.

In his autobiography of place, *The Lord's Woods,* Robert Arbib describes this form of perception at around the age of seven:

> Carl said I was crazy. How could something you couldn't see have a color? In the dark, my brown army blanket smelled blue, not brown at all. Old Mr. Wheeler down the street smelled blue, too. Like a penny, or a nail. Carl thought it was dumb. But to me, even sounds or letters came furnished with colors. One morning last year in third grade I told Miss Wilson that the letter S was blue. She asked me whether other letters had colors too. I told her that A was yellowy brown. (In *cat,* though, it was yellow.) I was silver. O was white, of course. U was gray. Everybody was laughing. Miss Wilson thought I was goofy. She didn't say so, but she stared at me for a long time and then turned her back to the class. I think she was crying, and I was sorry. (Even with my eyes closed, the woods smelled green, and always would.)

Werner's theory and Arbib's autobiographical description prompted me to listen more carefully to Tara's language. Sure enough, in addition to the visual metaphors described above, I noticed that she was also using cross-sensory metaphors. A year later, I captured these postnap comments:

SEPTEMBER 11, 1989 (2Y, 11M)   Tara comes downstairs after her nap. There had been a thunderstorm just as she was going to sleep. Tara reports, "I heard some pink thunder. Not soft, but a little loud."

> I ask, "What color is loud thunder?"
> "Avocado! Avocado green!"
> "Any other colors?"
> "Blue thunder is a little loud too."

This is clearly an example of chromesthesia. There's something about soft thunder that evoked pinkness for Tara. Going with the color idea she suggested, I explored to see if thunder can have other colors as well. Who would have imagined that loud thunder would be avocado green? But it makes sense—the dark, almost threateningly green quality of the skin of the avocado. Or perhaps she meant the intense yellow-green of the flesh. In either case, her comments made me realize that there is something about the intensity of avocado colors that is loud and perhaps a bit scary.

As parents and teachers we often struggle to get students to see the world metaphorically. We concoct exercises, using "right hemispheric" techniques to cultivate a different way of seeing. But rather than trying to teach something new, what we are really trying to do is uncover, or dust off, a facility for thinking and seeing that is inherent in early childhood. The process of understanding the world is, in part, one of making analogies between disparate things. The child is born with a metaphor-making capacity that facilitates leaps of imagination, the analogizing of bugs and jugglers, chainsaws and cheese, faces and airplanes.

As I became sensitive to Tara's metaphor making, I listened more carefully and learned to ask better questions. What color does that noise sound like? What animal does that person look like? Does this feel soft like sand or soft like a leaf? These questions took her natural tendency and extended it. I also tried to ask questions that encouraged organic metaphor making. Rather than prompting comparisons between natural and man-made things (this leaf looks like a shovel), I encouraged analogies between two natural things (this leaf looks like a grasshopper's wing). Following her lead, I tried to ground language in the images of the natural world.

Photosynthesis and Interdependence

Children's capacity to make connections also allows them to create unusual and telling ideas about ecological concepts. A striking example of Tara's intuitive ecological thinking came at the end of a long discussion when she was about three years old. Between ages two and six, more or less, Tara and I had a Saturday morning ritual that included sorting the recycling, loading up the trash, then driving to the dump–recycling center. She helped throw bottles in the recycling bins and was thrilled when she got to see the behemoth recycling truck drop off and pick up the immense thirty-foot bins. From the dump, we'd drive to a local farm to pick up creamy, unhomogenized, and unpasteurized milk. There we'd watch our friend Diana hand-milking the cows; then we'd pick up the Angora rabbits, feed apples to the horses or pigs, build forts in the hayloft, and ride the sheep. These encounters often led to talking about what animals eat and how we sometimes eat animals.

The following discussion, with its underlying emphasis on where things come from and where they go, emerged on one of those Saturday mornings. Over the preceding two weeks, there had also been some family discussion around where the poop goes when you flush the toilet. Wendy had said that the poop and the water go down through some pipes and into the backyard, out behind the barn, and into the leach field, where it gets made into new soil.

DECEMBER 9, 1989 (3Y, 2M)   Tara walks out of the house and sees exhaust coming out of the tailpipe of the truck. She inquires, "Daddy, is the truck making new soil?" I don't know if her reference is spawned by the notion of something coming out of a pipe making new soil or whether she is analogizing exhaust and poop. (A few days earlier, after I had told her not to stand in the exhaust because it would make her sick, Tara had asked, "Does the exhaust make the air sick?") In any case, the discussion leads to my making an analogy between us eating food and then pooping and the truck eating gasoline and then making exhaust, which is like poop.

Her question in response to this is, "Is it like sawdust?" She is associating what's left over after you cut wood with what's left over after you eat.

We get in the truck and are driving down the road. Some minutes have elapsed and I think the discussion is over, but then she asks, "Well, what do trees eat?"

I reply, "They drink water that they suck up from the ground."

"With their bottoms?" she says incredulously, thinking that this is different from what she does with her bottom.

"Yes, and they breathe air and eat things from the soil."

"But what do they eat from the soil?"

"Little things in the soil," I respond, not knowing how to be more descriptive.

"But *what* do they eat?" she demands insistently. She is getting frustrated with my oblique answers.

"Vitamins," I say finally, seizing on the closest parallel that I can find in her everyday experience to the raw materials that trees extract from the soil. This tangible image seems to quell her need for an answer. I can imagine her envisioning lots of little pills hidden in the soil. The trees reach out with the fingers of their root bottoms somehow and. . . .

Feeling successful with this explanation pulled from the empty hat of my mind, I forge ahead with the Golden Guide to photosynthesis. "And the neat thing is that we kind of share the air. The air we breathe out of our mouths, the trees breathe in with their leaves. And the air the trees breathe out of their leaves, we breathe in."

She considers that for a moment and then summarizes, "And so, there's a little bit of love between us and the trees."

This conversation seems striking at many levels. In the beginning, the analogies are flying a mile a minute. She associates exhaust and poop, herself and the air, then poop and sawdust. As we drive down the road, the unseen logic operating in her head is, "Well, if we eat and trucks eat, then trees must eat," which prompts her next question.

Second, I am struck by her persistence regarding what trees eat. "Little things" just didn't cut the mustard. Having entered into this discourse about what things eat and poop, she was intent on filling out the analogy with a concrete answer.

Her last comment really wowed me. It was as if it had dropped out of the collective unconscious and into her unsuspecting three-year-old mind. Yes, of course, I thought. How could we express this idea any more clearly? As John Muir said, "When we try to pick out anything by itself, we find it hitched to everything else in the Universe." But it took the naive wisdom of her young mind to make the final leap between these tangible, physiological connections and the binding love that unites all organisms.

What could be a better core principle for ecological living? Perhaps there's a little bit of love between all the organisms that breathe the same air in and out. Perhaps one of the tasks of parenting young children is cultivating their intuitive sense of unity. Before there are sharp distinctions between self and other, between me and everything out there, there's an intuition of inclusivity, of we're-all-in-this-together, trees and people and air and animals. Parents should encourage this sense of unity and interdependence as the foundation for later ecological thinking and environmental citizenship.

Talking Local

Some people would consider the previous conversation a good example of environmental education. After all, I did try to introduce the concept of photosynthesis. But while I am a firm believer in environmental education, those teaching it too often fall into the same trap as science educators. Teaching the value of salt marshes, or mineral recycling, to fourth graders is as problematic as teaching the contrasting particle and wave theories of light to seventh graders. These concepts as usually presented are prematurely abstract for the age of the children they are aimed at.

I have often encouraged parents and environmental educators to try to adjust their perspective. Instead of teaching "habitats" to third graders,

which requires grasping an unseeable assemblage of environmental vari-
ables, teach animal homes. Focus on nests—what they're made of and
how to make models of them. Too often, we skip the necessary primary
experience with the natural world and aspire to inculcate in children the
big conceptual ideas that we ourselves have grasped only as adults.

One of my favorite examples came from a Vermont mom who shared
with me a school project that her eight-year-old daughter had made. Her
daughter had been hard at work in her art studio out in the shed, and
appeared after an hour with an elegant poster to be displayed at the
general store next door. Around an attractive illustration read the bold
edict, conceived in all seriousness, "Save the Elephants. Don't Use Ivory
Soap!" It's easy to see how this young girl could make the mistaken connection between the killing of elephants for their ivory tusks and the
brand name of Ivory soap. This is what can happen when children are
confronted with political or social problems beyond the scope of their
comprehension.

The challenge is to prepare the fertile soil of the child's mind so that
ecological concepts germinate and flourish effortlessly. My argument
thus far suggests two avenues of thought. First, our explanations for
young children need to utilize metaphors, pictures and images, and stories. Second, ecological thinking, or systems thought, is intuitive. Young
children's thinking tends toward synthesis and integration through metaphoric analogizing. So, rather than teaching, we are supporting their
natural inclinations.

From feeling comfortable with children getting muddy, to encouraging children to handle worms and frogs or taste spinach fresh from the
garden, to supporting nature-based language and stories, the parent's objective should be to maximize a young child's sense of bondedness and
connection with the natural world. Rather than deluging them with facts
and environmental problems, we should be seeking accessible images
that help children start to grasp the big picture.

This next account illustrates Tara's solution to finding the right image
for an abstract concept: in this case, the water cycle. I have often railed

against the teaching of the water cycle to young children because it is usually done in a conceptually inaccessible fashion. I once worked with a group of fourth, fifth, and sixth graders who could all recite the water cycle forward and backward. To test their understanding I asked, "When it rains over the ocean, does it rain fresh or salt water?" Almost all of them were adamant that it rained salt water. Clearly, they didn't really understand the water cycle. These ideas are teachable and accessible, but only with a foundation of appropriate images and then a raft of tangible, concrete experiences to illustrate each element of the process.

In a conversation with Tara, an insight emerged out of walking in the neighborhood and talking about water:

APRIL 10, 1990 (3Y, 6M)   Tara, Eli, and I are walking back from our neighbor Mrs. Starr's house through the woods, a way we have never come before. We cross over a little stream, and I say that the big puddles in our backyard go through a pipe under our driveway and come down to this stream. Tara asks where it goes then. I say it goes down near our friend Solveig's house (about a half mile away) and then into a big stream, down to a river, and after a long trip into the ocean.

"Then it becomes clouds and rain and it falls into our backyard and goes down and around," I finish.

"Around and around?" Tara asks.

"Yes, just like that, around and around."

"Like a ring?" (I am not sure whether she's thinking of a wedding ring or ring-around-a-rosie, but both make sense.)

"Yes, we can call it the water ring."

She smiled and I could see the idea appealed to her.

That evening at bedtime we were looking at *Island Boy* by Barbara Cooney. It was too long and not really appropriate for her age, but we looked at the pictures and skimmed the story. It's about a boy who grows up on a Maine island, becomes an adult, and moves away to live on the mainland, but then, in his advanced years, comes back to the island. In the end, he dies and is buried on the island. Everyone comes to his funeral.

Tara asks, "What happens after he dies?"

My answer wasn't premade but created at the moment. "His body goes back into the earth to make new soil, and his spirit goes up into the sky to get ready to come back again."

"Like the water ring?"

"Yes, just like that."

Tara's final comment moved me for many reasons. First, I was enchanted by the simple elegance of the metaphor. Here was a set of appropriate images, built on each other, that offered a glimpse of understanding the water cycle and reincarnation. First, the "water ring" was created directly out of her experience in the neighborhood—playing in the backyard puddles, damming the water in the roadside ditch, walking home from Mrs. Starr's house. These concrete experiences, synthesized with a bit of her own language ("Like a ring?"), gave her a developmentally appropriate image for the water cycle. Then, with that image available to her, she could use it to make sense of other processes, like what happens when you die.

Something deep shifted inside me when she said this. Her mother and I had been puzzling about how we wanted to talk about death with Tara. We agreed that we wanted to convey a Buddhist perspective but hadn't settled on the wording. Not having read *Island Boy* before, I didn't realize it ended with a funeral and so hadn't decided ahead of time to distinguish between what happens to the body and to the spirit. But in responding to Tara's question, this distinction came to mind. I liked what I came up with, and moreover, it made sense to me. Her analogical leap to the water cycle, suggesting that the spirit flows around and around like the water, made the process of reincarnation seem natural rather than nonwestern and alien. It was soothing and familiar and it made me feel instantly more comfortable with my own fleetingness.

Finally, I sensed that this was an epiphany of what parenthood was all about—helping children make sense of the world in ways that are real but graceful, and being shaped, in return, by the child's wisdom.

For a long time after this, I don't have any references in my journal to cycles or the water ring. I vaguely recall wondering if the image had evaporated for her. Then, six months later, in early November, the image resurfaced.

Like many families, Wendy and I had a religious practice that was a loose amalgam of various eastern and western beliefs. We did not regularly attend church, but we aspired to develop a religious practice so that our children would feel a spiritual framework in our lives. We drew our inspiration from Buddhism and the earth-based Celtic and pagan seasonal celebrations of pre-Christian northern Europe. Trying to create a pattern for the spiritual year, we recognized the solstices and equinoxes as well as the cross-quarter days, the midpoints between each solstice and equinox (for example, Groundhog Day, which is also the Christian feast of Candlemas or the Celtic, pre-Christian observance called Imbolc). In our extended community, we usually took part in a bonfire celebration of the summer and winter solstices, and in our family we tried to find simple ways to mark the equinoxes and cross-quarter days.

The autumnal cross-quarter day, popularly celebrated as Halloween, is the eve of the Christian All Souls' Day, celebrated on the first of November and preserved in Mexico as the Day of the Dead. For this evening one year, Wendy created a set of rituals for us to try out. We had recently experienced several deaths in our families, and she was seeking a way to help resolve the sadness, so at dinner, in addition to the normal four place settings, she set a place for each departed soul. On each plate was a picture of one of our deceased family members—Wendy's father and mother, who had died when she was young, her sister, my sister, my mother, and my father, who had died just a few weeks earlier. For grace, we invited these loved ones to join us.

After dinner, in the darkness, Wendy and Tara went down to the frog pond by Mrs. Starr's house. Wendy put candles on pinecones, lit them, and floated them out on the black surface of the water. There were six candles, one for each departed soul in the family. As they sat watching the tiny flames floating in the darkness, Tara turned to Wendy and whispered, "The souls go around and around, you know."

Preserving Metaphoric Thinking

I believe that all children see the world metaphorically in ways similar to those revealed in my conversations with Tara. What's unusual about Tara is her articulate language at an early age. Some children walk early; some children talk early. Tara didn't really walk until about eighteen months, but she was clearly very verbal, very young. My son was the other way around: more physically adept and less verbally sophisticated, though he still expressed himself metaphorically on occasion.

So, though all young children think in images and metaphors, because some are not early talkers we don't always reap the benefit of their early thinking. By the time articulate language arrives, many of the unusual insights into early experience have receded. When early language overlaps with early experience, however, unexplored terrain is briefly revealed. The parenting challenge is to tune our ears to hear metaphoric language when it happens and incorporate it into our conversations with children. I noticed interesting examples when I was a preschool teacher, but I was usually so busy that I didn't manage to capture them in the net of my journal. In Tara's case, I had the time, inclination, and attentiveness to record her metaphor making.

Another factor that contributed to Tara's rich language was growing up in a TV-free home. She occasionally watched Saturday morning cartoons at a neighbor's house and was a video hound at friends' houses and on vacations. Like many young girls, she was enthralled by *The Little Mermaid, Bambi, Peter Pan,* and *The Nutcracker.* But for the most part, she spent her recreational time looking at books, listening to story tapes, dancing, drawing, and creating fantasy worlds. Free of the mind-numbing, time-consuming, and deteriorating effects of excessive television, her imagination had the opportunity to flourish.

In this kind of psychically unpolluted environment, I think it's more likely that organic metaphors will take root and flourish, grown with a minimum of additives and adulterations. What's appealing about the "water ring" notion is that it emerged, with a bit of nurturing, out of the fertile soil of Tara's own experience. The metaphor is physically grounded in her play experience and then is extracted and applied to other realms. Later on, she used the same image to explain her grasp of how library books go around and around through many people's hands. By supporting and using her own images, we helped her to create a sturdy metaphor, one that won't be uprooted by the storms of technological culture.

Just as we are becoming more sensitive to the virtues of nearby natural play and eating locally, I want to advocate for "talking local" with your children. By talking local, I mean two things. First, fill conversations with real, familiar natural objects rather than with references to television characters. Second, recycle the indigenous words and ideas children use and apply them in other contexts, as we did with Tara's water ring. Keep a journal, record your children's metaphors, and then use their unique local dialect to explain the world to them and to yourself. Spend time in the park talking about how the soft green of the grass is different from the glossy green of the rhododendrons and not at all like the avocado green of thunder. Encourage language that conveys that we are part of nature and it is part of us—that there is a little love between us and the trees, and maybe even the bees.

Deer Inside
Fostering an Alliance with Animals

In early childhood, empathy with animals is an inherent inclination. It's no accident that many characters in children's books aren't people. Famous animal characters inhabit *The Runaway Bunny, Winnie the Pooh,* and *Charlotte's Web,* to name just a few classics. Consider stuffed animals, petting zoos, and toddlers' squeals at squirrels. I remember the heartfelt horror when we lost Tara's favorite stuffed animal, Bun-bun, on a walk one day and had to launch a townwide search to get it back.

Joseph Chilton Pearce, author of *Magical Child,* contends that 80 percent of the characters in children's dreams are animals. And Paul Shepard, in *Arc of the Mind,* suggests that

> Animals have a magnetic affinity for the child, for each in its way seems to embody some impulse, reaction, or movement that is "like me." In the playfully controlled enactment of them comes a gradual mastery of the personal inner zoology of fears, joys, and relationships. In stories told, their forms spring to life in the mind, represented in consciousness, training the capacity to imagine.

Shepard contends that children are genetically programmed to relate to animals in order to support their cognitive and emotional development. Therefore, it's part of the role of the young child's parent to load this arc of the mind. This means reading stories about animals, providing opportunities to interact with animals, having animals around the house if possible, and "enacting," or becoming, animals. Outdoor play with my children was often structured around becoming animals. We walked like the fox, waddled like the porcupine, collected nuts like the gray squirrel, slid into ponds like otters. The goal was to be like them and learn their characters. In this way, "quick as a bunny," "wise as an owl," and "crafty as a fox" started to shape their personal inner zoologies.

I used this principle of befriending and becoming animals when Eli, at age two and a half, awoke at 4:15 on a September morning, stood up in his crib, and started to cry. This was unusual behavior for him; it was obvious he was very scared. I rose from bed quickly and went to him. After a minute or so, he started to explain voluntarily what was the matter.

"Deer inside. Deer inside. Deer in living room. I scared."

He was very upset. It's not unusual for young children to be afraid of big animals, however benign they may appear to adults.

"No, Eli. There's no deer. It's okay. There's nothing to be afraid of," I replied. But in doing so, I fell into the trap of refuting the child's dream experience, rather than accepting its emotional validity.

"Deer inside!" Eli insisted. "Deer go away?"

"Yes, it went outside," I said, now following his lead. Acknowledging and extending the dream imagery is a much more fruitful avenue when trying to soothe children. Though I know this deeply, my knee-jerk reactions are often more conventional.

"Deer go in woods?"

"Yes. The deer ran away into the woods." I had learned my lesson.

"Some guys scare deer away? Deer don't come back?"

"Yes. He won't come back."

"Feel better now." I was amazed that it was so easily resolved. He lay right down, I rubbed his back, and he was asleep in a few minutes.

We talked about the dream at breakfast. It was clear from his tone of voice that it was still very much on his mind. That night, to protect himself and keep the deer away, Eli wore his wolf shirt to bed. The deer didn't return that night, but he still kept talking about it the next day. "Deer come in bedroom, I scared," he would say, with a bit more wonder mixed in with his fear.

The next night after dinner, he crawled up into my lap. "Daddy, tell me a story." My personal storytelling challenge at this point was to make up stories on the spot, out of the particulars of the moment. It's like vernacular regional cuisine—you cook with what's immediately available in any given season. For instance, rather than today's burgers and pickles, salmon and peas used to be the traditional New England Fourth of July meal because salmon were running and the peas planted in early May were just plumping up. It's not always necessary to import dragons or Native American stories or Greek folklore if the raw materials are right at hand.

The Night Ride

I had been thinking about the deer dream and knew that I wanted to figure out a way to transform it into a less scary, more friendly experience. The dream had a potency and vividness that was valuable. Eli was both scared of, and in awe of, the deer in the living room. I wanted to reduce the fear and somehow build up the sense of alliance and closeness with the deer. Then I could use the dream to help knit his psychic life to our local wildlife. This is the story I told that evening:

One night, in the middle of the night, the little boy woke up. He heard a strange, thumpy noise. Was it his father turning over in the bed nearby? No, his father was snuggled under the quilt, not moving at all, fast asleep. He heard the thumpy noise again, over by the door to the living room. He looked over that way.

A big dark deer, with spreading antlers, stared at the little boy and stamped its foot again.

"I scared," whispered the little boy. He started to cry, wishing his Daddy would wake up.

The deer spoke in a low and warm voice.

"Don't be afraid, little boy. I won't hurt you." The deer lifted his legs up to his head, and with one twist and then another, removed his antlers and laid them down quietly on the floor. "I'm a friendly deer." The deer's big dark eyes smiled like his mother's eyes.

The deer crossed the room and stood by the little boy's crib. "Quietly, quietly, climb on my back. Don't wake your Daddy from his deep, sleepy nap."

As the deer leaned over, the little boy put his arms around the deer's neck and pulled himself up. The deer slipped across the room and out the front door.

"Hold on tight with all your might," the deer whispered as they bounded down the road. The little boy laid his cheek against the warm fur of the deer and laughed in the wind.

Down the road, through the woods, on the trail, to the falls. The deer's hooves splooshed in the mud by the little stream, but the little boy stayed warm and dry, up high on the deer's back. The deer sipped a drink at the waterfall and bounded on. On to a trail the little boy had never walked on. To a cathedral of pines by the edge of the lake.

They stopped where the moonlight streamed off the water. The boy felt the deer panting beneath him. Slipping his legs over to one side, he dropped down to the ground. A mother deer and two fawns, curled in a circle, looked up at him.

"Children, here's your wish. A friend to play with," said the father deer. The little boy followed the fawns to a big pile of leaves in the woods. They bounced in the pile; leaves scattered everywhere. They tickled and giggled; leaves crunched in their hair.

They ran back to the mother and father deer, and the fawns all pleaded, "Please, Daddy, can we keep him?" But the little boy thought of riding in the truck with his father, taking a bath with his mom, jumping on the couch with his sister, and he felt sad.

"I miss *my* family. I want to go home."

The mother deer licked his nose and he clambered up to ride home on her back. Down the path through the woods, past the waterfall falling, up the hill to the house, to his family all asleep.

The mother deer eased the door open with her nose, tiptoed past his sleeping daddy, and slipped him into the crib. "Please come in bed with me," he whispered. She climbed in next to him and the little boy spooned up next to her warm tummy. When he was asleep, she crept out the door and disappeared in the darkness.

In the morning time, the little boy woke up. "Daddy, come in bed with you?" His father scooped him up and into his bed. They sang "The Wheels on the Bus" and "Zip-a-Dee-Doo-Dah" until they heard the little boy's sister come down the creaky stairs and open the door to the bedroom. "Why are there deer footprints on the rug?" she wondered in a sleepy voice. And the little boy remembered and chirped, "Daddy, deer inside last night. But I not scared."

The Tale Becomes a Tail

This turned out to be just the first in a series of stories. In each of them, Eli went off to spend time in the woods with the deer, and eventually he was transformed into one. He roamed with bobcats, fishers, and porcupines; he was pursued by hunters; he felt the hunger pangs of winter. I used this set of stories to introduce him to deer natural history, predator-prey relationships, and ethical issues about hunting.

During one particularly suspenseful adventure, he barely made it to the portal from the deer world back into our neighborhood. He had to slip through a slender passageway between two large oaks to get transformed from a deer back into a boy. He slipped through just in the nick of time, but because he was a second late he was left with a fawn's tail. This story, being told as we drove home one evening, ended just as we pulled into our driveway. He begged for me to continue the story, but I declined. Too late, time for dinner.

As we walked toward the house, I remembered that the cat had left a chipmunk's tail on the patio the night before, and I had put it on the patio table. Now I surreptitiously grabbed the tail and tucked it into Eli's belt without his realizing what I was doing. When his sister asked him why he had a little tail, he whirled around to see it drooping over his bottom. His face registered wonder and amazement. I exclaimed, "Oh, my gosh! The story must be true. You just barely made it back from being a fawn." For the longest time, he partly believed that the transformation had really happened.

Dreams that are transformed into stories can rekindle new dreams and be powerful creators of personal lore and values. And the ability to imagine oneself transformed into another creature, feeling its pain and pleasures from the inside, is a unique capacity of early childhood. While the differentiation between subject and object is still casual, while the boundaries are permeable, we want children to move easily back and forth. When children play at being a deer, they become the deer, living the experience from the inside out.

My goal with the deer stories, and other stories that followed, was to create a foundational empathy between my children and other creatures. This serves at least two purposes. For Eli, it brought a little bit of animal wildness into his body and soul. I hoped it made him feel sleek, powerful, able to bound surefootedly through the woods. I also felt that, later on, his empathy with animals could be transformed into a desire to protect their habitats and eventually into a commitment to preserve the natural world.

I sensed that this empathic disposition had stuck when Eli, at age eleven, described a dream in which he became Gwinna, the family dog:

> I opened my eyes and I was looking at Mommy's knees and I couldn't figure out where I was, and then I started lapping up some water and I realized I was Gwinna. It felt so good to be able to run so fast, and the smells were really strong, and when somebody told me to sit, my back legs just went down, zoom, like I didn't have any choice.

What fascinated me about this description was that Eli discovered dog perception and experience in ways that surprised him. He hadn't thought about how it would feel to be in a dog's body when it responded to a command. In the dream, it just happened. The dream transformation gave him that insight, allowing him to see and feel the world through a dog's body and eyes.

And at thirteen, after a day of fishing with his friend Julian, Eli reflected, "You're swimming along, it's all blue and green, you chomp on a bug, then you're yanked up, your mouth stings, it's blindingly bright, and *whomp*, your life gets smacked out of you. It's unfair!" At that point, Eli was kissing fish before throwing them back. He is still mostly a catch-and-release fisherman, unless he's bringing them home for me to eat.

If we seek emotional intelligence and ecological literacy for our children, we have an unusual opening in their early childhood. Later in life we may try for ourselves to develop the ability to see things from someone else's perspective, to stand in another's shoes. The Night Ride story sequence was a first playful step toward fostering Eli's development of the skill of empathy, which later would help him with the spiritual challenge of letting go of ego, of stepping outside of himself. If young children can feel comfortable moving back and forth between self and animal, between indoors and outdoors, then those pathways are easier to follow later in life. The simple act of play naturally wears the paths into the landscape.

Moon–Jumping Nights
Reanimating the Natural World

Luckily, the townwide search for Tara's beloved stuffed bunny paid off. Someone found him on the side of the road, noticed our poster on a telephone pole, and called so that we could reunite Tara and Bun-bun. The homecoming was festive. Tara asked where he'd been and, of course, we provided Bun-bun's responses in bunny voices. Perhaps it seems a bit silly from an adult perspective to put so much energy into the sham of a stuffed animal being alive. But it's important to recognize the intuitive behavior of young children and speculate about its potential usefulness.

Dolls and stuffed animals are easily animated by the young child. In the Night Ride stories I told Eli, all the deer family members spoke proper English, and the ability of animals to talk was never questioned. Not just animals, but natural phenomena and other wonders of the physical world can be easily personified by young children. Sticks readily become snakes or horses. Young girls often develop close relationships with trees, with whom they have conversations and confide their deepest secrets.

This tendency is often compared to Native Americans' investing the wind or the flowers with sentient qualities. While we acknowledge and accept this tendency as charming or endearing, we tend to conceive of it as a primitive attitude, a characteristic of minds not yet trained to objectify or acclimated to the structure of the real world. But with new interest in the concept of Gaia—the planet as a self-regulating, metabolic organism—it may be time to reevaluate our attitude toward personifying the natural world. I contend that such animation of the natural world, along with the anthropomorphizing of animals, is an important step toward ecological consciousness.

When my children personified nonhuman things, I tried to support and encourage this "misconception." Some people feel that this misleads the child into false views of the world, like the myth of Santa Claus that falls apart at age nine. When they discover that Santa doesn't really exist, some children are crestfallen and brokenhearted. Wouldn't it be better not to cultivate the fantasy in the first place? As regards Santa, I still haven't made up my mind. But as regards the natural world, the answer is clear to me. Personifying aspects of nature is a way of creating living bonds with an ecosystem. If children feel that the wind, earth, and water are their "friends," then they will feel a protective commitment to them as they mature.

Brooke Herter, in an unpublished essay on what she calls "moon jumping," describes a memory from age six when her mother would rouse her and her sister in the middle of the night to dance in the light of the full moon. Her mother awakens the girls, invites them out onto the moonlit, dewy grass, and watches from the door. She describes:

> My mother at the door, framed in the moonlight, bridging the world of home-safeness with the reign of moon-magic. We jump and run, backwards and forwards, rolling over, never touching, but always entwined by a triangular thread that embraces each other and our home.

Later, back in bed, as her mother leaves:

She is gone, down the hall, leaving a smell of freshness and evening lingering by my pillow. But the moonshine stays till my eyes close. Playing in my room, waking the books and stuffed animals with its touch. I feel intrigued, small; I think I have a friend in the moonshine, but I'm not sure.

Musing on the significance of these experiences, Herter explains,

In recalling my moon-jumping sojourns of the night . . . I am reminded of the absolute wonder of those evenings. As a child, I had no words to describe the largeness of the moon, the deepness of the night, or the sweetness of the air. But I had a child's knowledge of an everlasting pact, friendship, bond between myself and the natural world.

Through fostering this "friendship" with the moon, Herter's mother created a bond between Brooke and the natural world.

Tara, at around age three, also made friends with the moon, a natural inclination I happily encouraged and one that grew into a more elaborate kind of personification. As we were driving back from a wedding at the end of August, Tara started talking to the full moon. It felt completely natural for me to respond to her in the moon's voice—low, soothing, and perhaps a little grandmotherly. The moon asked her about her day and she responded chattily, looking at and addressing her comments to the moon.

Inspired by Jane Yolen's wonderful book *Owl Moon*, Tara and I developed a tradition of going out to call in owls on full-moon nights, where Tara's relationship with the moon took on a functional value.

NOVEMBER 11, 1989 (3Y, 1M)   It is warm and blustery tonight, and Tara and I go owling. We walk along the road to the Monadnock-Sunapee trail and then turn up the path through the woods. Tara walks most of the way up, until a thick patch of darkness ahead of us scares her. Then I pick her up. At the waterfall, Tara talks to the moon.

"It's kind of scary out here in the darkness," she begins.

I reply as the moon: "Oh, I'll protect you, and there are lots of friendly animals around. Deer and rabbits and skunks. . . ."

"I have a skunk hat!" Tara is referring to the hat she is wearing, which is a fanciful interpretation of a skunk's head.

"It looks so soft," answers the moon. "If I had hands, I could reach down and touch it."

"Well, I could glue hands on you." Tara reaches up and makes some gluing motions with her hands in the air. "There, I did it."

"Great! I'm reaching down and feeling your soft hat, and here's a soft moon kiss for you."

My objective, though I wasn't clear about this when we started the moon discussions, was to have Tara experience the moon as her friend. This way, I hoped, she would feel accompanied and not alone in the dark. Starting with her native tendency to talk to the moon, to imbue it with consciousness and personality, I encouraged a relationship that was soothing and reassuring. I was motivated in part by a vividly re-membered experience from when I was twelve years old, of being out in the night looking for something lost. Huddled in the bushes, scrabbling in the leaves, I suddenly realized, "I'm not afraid of the dark." Instead of the anxious emptiness in the pit of my stomach that I normally felt at night, I felt embraced and softly held by the darkness. The darkness, and the wild unfamiliarity of the woods, by association, felt less alien and more accessible. I hoped that I could encourage this same feeling in Tara's relationship to the dark aspects of the natural world by extending her instinctive inclination to personify the moon.

A Council of All Beings

An event from later in Tara's third year shows her ease at personifying other natural phenomena:

SEPTEMBER 19, 1990 (3Y, 11M)   We are driving back from Peterborough and I start talking about how foggy it is. Tara wants to know what fog is, and I say it's when clouds get sleepy and they come down to rest on the ground. She thinks about this and asks with a giggle, "The clouds think Mother Earth is their pillow?"

In this situation, I intentionally guided her with a metaphor of my own. From experience, I have learned that these kinds of explanations are accessible to children. One starts from known concepts (clouds, getting sleepy, lying down for a nap) and assembles them to create a new understanding. I personified clouds by saying they get sleepy, knowing that this familiar concept can engage children's empathy. Even so, Tara's question adds a kind of comfortable grace to the picture. Her image suggests an intuitive friendliness between clouds and the earth that I had never perceived. Whereas I have seen clouds and the earth as related elements of a natural system, I had not considered them as cuddling up with each other.

This next account blends personification with the kind of deep empathy that children have with animals, akin to the examples from Eli's life in the previous chapter. As skittish animals will often flock to children, so children flock emotionally to animals, even cold-blooded ones.

DECEMBER 23, 1989 (3Y, 3M)   We stop at the Peterborough Fish Market and Tara looks in the display cases. There is a platter of whole, un-cleaned trout. Their unlidded eyes stare blankly, their mouths agape as if they died in midsentence. Tara blurts out, "Those fish aren't happy! Why are they in there? Why are they dead? They want to be swimming around in the water."

In the car, as we drive away, she is very insistent. "I feel sad about the fish." And she starts to sob. Not just crying but deep, racking sobs of swollen emotion. Her sobbing is so heartfelt that I feel teary myself. I try to explain that the fish give themselves to us so we can eat them, but she insists that they don't want to be dead, that they want to be swimming around in the water. It's hard to refute her conviction.

Some six months later a related discussion took place. I do not recall or have any journal entries about intervening discussions on the topic of fish.

JULY 13, 1990 (3Y, 9M)   After seeing a production of *Alice in Wonderland* in Robin Hood Park, Tara and I are riding home in the car. Spontane-ously she initiates a conversation unrelated to anything I can remember in the last six hours: "Isn't it sad when fish die? Why do they have to die?" It is evident she has been thinking about this, and I can foresee the day when she will not want to eat fish. I say that sometimes it makes me sad, but I also like to eat fish. When I say that the fish become part of us, our skin, our hands, when we eat them, it makes it better somehow. She laughs and smiles at this silly and happy idea.

Inherent in this sympathy for fish are, I think, the seeds of a fundamental respect for all beings. The Buddhist writer Joanna Macy's concept of a council of all beings aspires to promote a deep affinity between people and all organisms we share the planet with. We should respect not only the cuddly or charismatic mammals but also the creepier, less human lifeforms such as bugs and horseshoe crabs and fish. (I'm still working on my attitude toward ticks, but I haven't made much progress.) The deep ecology movement encourages humans to recognize the integrity of *all* species. My sense is that this is an old rather than a new understanding, from both a species and an individual development perspective. It was the mind-set of our genetic forebears, the hunter-gatherers, and it is an intuition of young children to sense the camaraderie between people and other organisms.

Trusting that Tara's inclinations and feelings are representative of young children, I conclude that this empathy extends to nonliving phenomena such as the moon and the clouds. As the metaphoric tendency of early childhood bridges the gap between images and concepts in language, it also bridges the gap between unlike aspects of creation and creates a kind of intraplanetary empathy. Cultivating this empathy in early childhood is one of the foundations of living lightly on the planet. Building such bonds not only instills an environmental ethic but also helps young children see all parts of the world as an extended family. Perhaps even the threatening darkness of the night, the dwelling place of all things scary and dangerous, can be experienced as a soft blanket of familiarity.

A Mouthful of Flowers

Toward the end of her third year, Tara started to recount, completely of her own accord, her experiences with fairies and angels. Our initial response was to be open-minded about this relationship and to accept and inquire about her experiences with casual interest.

Imaginary friends are a well-documented phenomenon in early childhood, tending to appear around age three or four and take their leave around six or seven. Much has been made of their function in the developing ego of the child; they often serve as playmates for solitary children, and outdoor play seems to support their appearance. Of course, fairies, elves, and their kin are most often creatures of the wood and wild, appearing in far-flung cultures around the world. Although the sources of belief in such imaginary beings are different, a child's openness to them is similar to her openness to relationships with animals or the moon.

A world of mystery and magic exists alongside our everyday world, and its boundaries are permeable to young children. They haven't yet walled off human beings as an isolated clan. So it seemed a quite understandable step when Tara moved from personifying the inanimate moon or stuffed bunny to creating invisible beings. When these creatures appeared, I tried to stay open to the notion that my children were sensing some hidden aspect of a parallel reality that I had lost the ability to see or understand. I took comfort in knowing that many adults remember vividly the appearance and character of the imaginary friends that were part of their early childhood.

To a certain extent we gently supported the possible existence of these life-forms. A simple straw angel hung from a beam in Tara's room to watch over her at night. We read the Flower Fairy books to her, and we built fairy houses with both her and Eli. There was a period when the children built fairy houses in a mossy patch under the oak tree in the backyard. They'd leave presents for the fairies, and Wendy and I, acting as fairy surrogates, would exchange them with simple presents for Tara and Eli. (Eli recently told me that he and Tara started to suspect this ruse, so they built a different fairy house, left presents, and didn't tell us. A couple of days later, those presents had been replaced by others—left by fairies? I have no explanation.)

In any case, we cultivated the fairy fantasy in the same spirit of ani-

mating the natural world, of encouraging a belief in the aliveness of creatures and forces, real and imagined, all around us.

Tara's accounts of her meetings with fantasy creatures had a matter-
of-fact quality to them:

SEPTEMBER 11, 1989 (2Y, 11M)   We wake up in the morning to find a
dead frog the cats had dragged into the kitchen. On the way to preschool Tara says, "I was walking down the road and I found a dead
angel lying in the road," in her very serious, straight-ahead tone of
voice. I suspect that the dead frog and the dead angel are related, but
I never figure this out.

SEPTEMBER 13, 1989 (2Y, 11M)   At dinner, Wendy and I are trying to
catch our five minutes of daily conversation before Eli starts scream-
ing or the phone rings. Tara interrupts and with no introduction says,
"I was walking in the road, going to pick blueberries, and I met an
angel and she wanted to eat blueberries but she couldn't because her
mouth was full of flowers."

Something about this image had the ring of genuineness. I couldn't
recall any examples of "mouths full of flowers" in Tara's experience. It
seemed to be something she had actually come upon, at least in her vivid
imagination, like a striking dream image that unfolds independent of
conscious will.

For the next six months, Tara's fairies and angels remained generic;
no specific personalities emerged. Then, about a week before we departed for a family trip to California, Tara started talking about playing with
Annie. Sometimes Annie was a fairy, sometimes an angel, sometimes a
fairy-angel. Annie accompanied us to California and was a dependable
playmate while we were there. Wendy and I both thought it was an interesting coincidence that Annie was the name of Wendy's sister who had
died about eight years earlier and who had lived in California. Wendy
and her sister had been exceptionally close.

After we returned from California, Tara's descriptions of Annie became more and more explicit:

JUNE 19, 1990 (3Y, 8M)   Putting Tara to bed tonight, we look at a book, turn out the light, and then, on a whim, I ask about Annie.

"Where does Annie sleep?"

Tara says, "Up on the roof."

"Does she go out through the window?"

"Yeah, well, you know, she folds up her wings and puts them in a pocket. Like on the airplane when the wheels go inside a pocket, Annie pushes a button on her head and her wings go inside."

"Does she push the button again to make the wings come out?"

"No, she pushes a different button on her arm," Tara replies.

Three weeks later Tara offered an explanation of the relationship between fairy-angels and the natural world:

AUGUST 21, 1990 (3Y, 11M)   At dinner, pretty much out of nowhere, Tara announces spontaneously, "The trees are really angels. A long time ago you could talk to the angels in lots of ways, but now they hide in trees."

Wendy quizzes her: "Did someone tell you that?" (We both suspected that this comment could have come from Tara's Waldorf-trained preschool teacher. We later checked and it didn't.)

Tara shakes her head. "No, because I know myself how the angels live and be."

Tara delivered that last comment with an uncanny assuredness and authority in her voice. When she talked about these phenomena, it sounded like firsthand knowledge or direct experience. It was hard to ascertain if Tara was "just making things up" or having some kind of imagined experience—or even having some kind of real experience that was inaccessible to adult consciousness.

The conventional explanation would be to consider Tara's fairy-angels a subset of imaginary friends, beings constructed completely in the young child's active imagination and having no objective existence. Conversely, perhaps imaginary friends are a subset of fairy-angels. Perhaps children really are regularly befriended by beings that we adults have lost contact with. I am reminded of the characterization of angels in Wim Wenders's

film *Wings of Desire*. In this movie, angels exist all around us and fleet-
ingly make their presence known to adults in times of stress and dire
need. Certainly the notion of the guardian angel pervades much of Christian culture. Perhaps children's minds, "un-adulterated" by conventional
thought patterns, perceive these beings easily.

Regardless, it was clear to me that something valuable was happening
for my children out there in the backyard and in the neighborhood. The
ability to play freely in a safe meadowy and forested landscape allowed
Tara and Eli to experience the aliveness of the natural world. Trees became things to climb, horses to ride, hiding places for fairies. The day-
lilies, garden vegetables, and stone walls weren't just things but creatures
with daily lives, wants and needs, feelings and yearnings. All of them had
a voice, even if their mouths were sometimes full of flowers.

Parents can help give voice to the mute or imaginary creatures in
their child's nearby world. It's a challenging game to come up with different voices for the full moon and the waning crescent, the owl and the
pussycat. Through being encouraged to hold conversations with nature's
creations, children start to develop the skill of taking another person's
perspective. And might not a relationship with fairies prepare us for welcoming the numinous or the spiritual into our lives, an unseen presence
that exists just beyond the edge of the visible world?

Environmental educators are catching on, too. Environmental centers
with an appreciation for imaginary play in nature are creating programs
that cultivate a sense of wonder. For three weeks prior to the Midsum-
mer's Eve celebration at the Minnetrista Cultural Center in Muncie, In-
diana, a dancer trains local children to develop a flower fairy persona.
Each child chooses a flower, learns its attributes, and devises a movement
repertoire and a costume based on the flower's attributes. At the summer
solstice, the community is invited to stroll the brick pathways through
the preserved Victorian gardens of the Ball Estate, where candlelit paths
offer glimpses of flower fairies frolicking amid the blooms. These children may look back on the experience as a gift that helped them feel at
home in the night garden of the natural world.

The Mermaids and the Necklace
Magical Realism as a Family Art

"*Tell us a story, Daddy.*" It was a constant refrain that I treated as a personal challenge. Part of me always resisted, felt tired, didn't want to rise to the task. On the other shoulder was my better self, the self that realized that our family storytelling tradition was creating a rich, almost mythological tapestry unique to our family and place. Just as aboriginal Australians record their ancestral history in songs and pathways through the bush, I was creating a body of folklore that preserved our family culture, our stories in our places. I sensed there was something powerful here, so when coaxed, I tried to move through the hesitancy and into story space.

The Night Ride stories with Eli used his dream, and the trails, pine groves, and ponds around our house as raw material. This became the operative principle: start stories from the serendipitous particulars of the time, place, and people of the moment. When my children said, "Tell us a story, " I often tried to make one up on the spot, with no prior preparation, so that I'd be most likely to access the freshest, most immediate layer of our shared experience. The story would begin in the present and gradually take on its own shape and form.

And it was crucial that the stories took place in the natural world. Home is knowable and predictable, whereas the woods, gorge, marshes, and meadows are mysterious and uncertain. The developmental challenge, as children move from early to middle childhood, is for them to venture out into unknown landscapes to forge their own path. Tara and Eli were always entranced by my story explorations, and I have come to see them as one of the crucial elements of parenting children into nature. The stories affirmed the value of learning about the creatures, plants, and bedrock of the surrounding world. They helped prepare our children to explore first the natural world and then broader cultural worlds, providing maps Tara and Eli would follow in pursuing their individuation.

This kind of story is like the path that diverges from the road through the woods. The road is level and predictable, wide and comfortable. As you branch off onto the story path, you can still see the main road and will rejoin it farther along, but it gradually disappears from view as the path seeks elevation, narrows, and twists through an unexpected forest. The story explores new terrain, discovers talking animals in the woods. Eventually the road reappears through the mist, the landscape looks familiar again, and soon you're back with the road securely beneath your feet.

The Mermaids and the Necklace

For about three summers, when Tara was about four to six years old and Eli was two to four, we took a summer vacation at a house on a lake in western Maine. Craig and Sarah, our friends who owned the house, had three daughters close in age to our children. There was a big main house with a deck, a tiny beach, a dock for jumping off, and a float. A charming cabin right on the water served as our family's sleeping quarters.

We engaged in a swirl of activities. Swimming, building sand castles, feeding the ducks, and cooking out. Visits to the maze of pathways in the woods, blueberrying and blackberrying, excursions to the big sand beach with the stream. Motorboating, canoeing, sailing, rafting, water-skiing, and paddleboating. Imagine the curlicue ride when we took the motorboat out in the middle of the lake and turned the wheel over to a three-year-old. But best of all were the quiet times, the moments of repose. There was ample time for silliness and for stories, to start a story and tell it over a couple of days, or to sow the seeds of a story and let it grow up and outward.

One breathless and soft afternoon, I was swimming from the float back to the beach with Tara, age five, and Marta, age three, on an inflatable raft . Nearby was a rock where a mother merganser and her eight ducklings sometimes rested when the kids weren't feeding them bread crumbs at the beach. We had been eyeing the duck rock as a swimming destination for a couple of days, and Tara requested that we go there now. On the rock, the girls leaned back on their hands, stretched their legs out, and sunned themselves. No breeze stirred the surface of the water. "Tell us a story, Daddy."

One velvety summer afternoon, two young mermaids are stretched out on the rocks. They lean back their heads, letting their hair dangle just above the water, and they feel the sun warm their tails. The waves lap ever so gently on the rock and they are lulled to sleep. They wake up with a start! Something is wrong. All their necklaces, bracelets, and rings are gone—someone has stolen them. Swimming away toward the beach is a blond-haired boy wearing a pink bathing suit. "Stop!" they shout. "Bring back our jewelry!" But he doesn't listen. He surges out of the water and runs into the cabin by the water's edge where he sleeps at night. When he comes out, he no longer has the mermaids' jewels in his hands.

The mermaids are sad and angry. He had no right to take their jewels! They want to go to the cabin and get them back, but they can't walk on the land. They don't know what to do.

After a while the mother duck and her ducklings swim to the rock. Seeing tears on the mermaids' faces, she asks them what is wrong. "That little boy stole our jewelry and we can't get it back!" The mother duck is thoughtful and then says, "Perhaps I can help you. I have a plan." The mermaids had once saved one of her baby ducklings from drowning when its leg got stuck on a branch underwater, and the mother duck wants to return their kindness. The mermaids explain where they think the little boy hid the jewels, and the ducks go on their way.

The children finish swimming and are getting ready for supper when the mother duck brings her ducklings to the beach for their evening snack. All the children run down to the beach, laughing and tossing cracker crumbs into the water. The little boy in the pink bathing suit loves feeding the ducks. Because there are so many, no one notices when the mother duck swims away, slips into the bushes, and secretly waddles over to the little boy's cabin. She pushes open the screen door with her bill, hops inside, and starts looking as fast as she can for the jewels. She finds them stuffed under a pillow, scoops them all up in her beak, and waddles quickly back into the water.

The mermaids have been watching from the water shadows, and they swim to the rock to meet the duck. They are overjoyed! They put on all their jewelry, splash happily in the water, thank the duck, and return to their home in the depths of the lake. The mother duck collects her ducklings from the beach. And the little boy never figures out what happened to all those jewels.

The girls knew right away that the culprit was Eli. Many sibling squabbles took just this form: "Eli took my _____." The girls easily saw themselves as the mermaids, and they recognized the ducks and the cabin at the water's edge. I structured the story with numerous points of familiarity so as to make the story events seem recognizable. The entrance to Narnia through the wardrobe, the magical folded into the ordinary, is a traditional story motif. But this episode with the ducks is but one piece of the tale that was taking shape.

The next day we paddled down the lake for a visit to the Enchanted Woods, a remarkable place that the children and I looked forward to visiting every summer. It was a handmade theme park in miniature where, on ten acres of ordinary coniferous and hardwood forest, innumerable trails wove around and over little streams to the Gnome Forest, Hernando's

Hideaway, the Witch's Den, the lofty Clubhouse, the Turkey Chute (a long slide among the trees), and other structures set in grottos, nooks, and dells. This private and completely unheralded endeavor was a unique expression of eccentric American folk art based purely on childhood fantasy and magic. Quietly, a couple and their two children had dedicated their summers to creating this retreat for themselves and extended family.

The sensitive parents who created this wonderland took all the most compelling childhood fantasies and gave them scintillating scaffolding. All children want to sneak into the witch's cabin in the dark woods. Here they can actually do it. Everyone fantasizes about being one of Peter Pan's lost children. Here they can become one of them. Open a doorway in the side of an old maple and, if you are child-sized, you can climb up a ladder *inside* the tree to the woodpecker's perch twenty feet off the ground. Find the all-seeing crystal in the wizard's house nestled into the roots of an old hemlock. Or ride the airplane, suspended ten feet above the forest floor, almost two hundred feet through a copse of spruces.

On this particular day, many summers ago, Captain Hook's pirate ship captured everyone's interest. This boat, tossed far from shore by a fluke wind, didn't look like a play structure at all. First of all, it was big, maybe twenty-five feet from end to end, a scaled-down pirate vessel complete with large steering wheel, cannons, and a rope swing so Peter Pan and his merry band could swing on board. Using swords, eye patches, Hook's hook, Tiger Lily's headband, and a jar of fairy dust extracted from the old sea chest, the children rampaged around the deck. They discovered the hatch to go belowdecks and found—lo and behold!—a treasure chest tucked away in a hidden corner. Sparkling jewels, silver pieces, necklaces, and gold doubloons spilled over the edges as the girls opened the top. When it was time to leave, I had to peel Tara away from the treasure chest. Normally an honest child, she tried to surreptitiously slip a rhinestone necklace into her pocket and was crestfallen when I told her to put it back.

That evening, she reminisced wistfully about the treasure. A seed of story elaboration started to germinate in my mind.

Elaborating and Inhabiting the Story

The next day the skies opened up and it poured, forecasting a dreary day inside with kids getting on each others', and our, nerves. We decided to take the kids to Bridgton to see the film *101 Dalmatians*. Tara had seen it about a month earlier but was raring to go again. I had never seen it and was dismayed by how violent it was.

After the movie, the rain slowed to a drizzle. While Sarah kept the girls occupied with a klatch of downtown ducks and geese, I did a quick tour of the antique shops. In a corner of one shop, jumbled in a paper bag, was some dusty costume jewelry. For two dollars I got a string of simulated pearls with a rhinestone pendant in the center, two tiny loops of pearls that hung down, and a large clasp workable by small fingers. It was just like the jewels in the treasure chest, and, though the plan was still only a glimmer, I sensed that this was just the kind of thing that mermaids would wear.

I knew I wanted to create some kind of treasure hunt, solvable by Tara, that would challenge her developing sense of the landscape around the house and cabin, but the details were not yet clear.

Two afternoons later, when everyone was occupied but Tara, I sensed the time was right and dashed across the road to where three paths head up into the woods. One path goes through an elegant stand of large white pines, with lots of thick moss underneath but no underbrush, which we called the Mossy Woods. Another leads to the maze, a network of paths in a dense red pine plantation. The third goes only a short way and then stops. In the Mossy Woods, there is a memorial stone and an old, lichen-encrusted wooden bench. I wrapped the necklace in oak leaves and hid it under the bench, making it barely visible if you were standing next to it.

As I walked back to the house, I tried to figure out how I was going to get Tara up there. She'd been on those paths a few times, so I thought she knew her way around. But how would I present the clues, or explain the existence of the necklace? In the proverbial flash, my plan jelled.

Back at the house, I told Tara that I'd had a special dream the night before and I wanted to tell her about it. We went for a bike ride and looked for a special place, good for telling dreams, and finally agreed on a little piece of abandoned asphalt road. Moss and shrubs grew in from the sides and a canopy of branches created an open but cozy spot underneath.

"Tell me about the dream right now, Daddy!" she demanded.

Last night I dreamt that I swam out to the duck rocks and I was surprised to find the mermaids there. The mermaids said they were so overjoyed to get their jewelry back that they neglected to notice that one necklace was missing. They asked the mother duck to go look for it, but when she went to the cabin, the little boy was leaving. The duck could see a little piece of the necklace peeking out of his pocket, so she followed him.

The little boy took the necklace to a pine forest and hid it under a bench near a big patch of moss. The duck hid in the woods, waited for the boy to leave, and was going to retrieve the necklace when she noticed a fox lurking nearby. She didn't want to be eaten, so she hightailed it back to the lake and told the mermaids what she had seen.

Since the mermaids had never been up on the land, they didn't know the place that the duck was describing. They did know that they didn't want that little boy to keep their necklace. The mermaids said to me, "Find the necklace in the moss so deep, then surely it is yours to keep." I thanked them, swam back to the beach, and then I woke up.

At the point in the dream where I described the hiding place, Tara's eyes got wide. She inhaled sharply and grabbed my arm. As soon as I was finished she said, "Daddy! I know where that is!"

"Really? I've been thinking about it and I can't figure it out."

"It's where that big gravestone is in the Mossy Woods!" she said excitedly.

"But I don't remember a bench there." At this point I was both challenging her memory and trying to make this more of a puzzle to solve.

"Yes, there is, right nearby!"

"I thought it might be where we set up the tents underneath the trees." This was disinformation on my part. This second place fit the description, and I wanted her to search and be thwarted first before getting to the right spot. "There's a big patch of moss there, and you brought out a little bench from the house."

"That's right," Tara agreed. "We can look in both spots."

"You know, this is just a dream," I cautioned. "I don't know if there's a real necklace. Sometimes dreams are true, and sometimes they're not. We might look and look for a necklace and not find anything."

"I know, but let's go look right now!"

Her excitement was electric as we pedaled back to the house. On arriving, she dashed over to the tents and searched all around the bench. Finding nothing, she was disappointed but still fired up. She wanted to go to the Mossy Woods. I let her lead the way up the driveway to the road, feigning ignorance about directions.

"Now where do we go?" I inquired. She walked along the road, evaluating the options, and headed straight up the correct path, into the Mossy Woods. In a few minutes, the clearing appeared. She caught a glimpse of the stone and charged over. "See? Here's the bench!" She glanced under the bench and, finding nothing, became disappointed, but I encouraged her. "Remember I said how sometimes dreams aren't true, but if it is true, I bet that little boy would hide the necklace very carefully."

She got down on her hands and knees and ran her hands under the bench until they hit the leaf package. A few pearls slipped into view. "It's here!" she gasped, cupping the necklace lovingly in her hands. Though I don't often recollect conversations word for word, her next comment was so striking that I remember the phrasing exactly. "Oh, Daddy, this makes my heart feel inspired."

We walked back to the house and she immediately went to find Eli. "Eli, is this your necklace?" she demanded, attempting, I think, to confirm the authenticity of the story and the dream. Yes, Eli said, smiling and nodding compliantly, though of course he had absolutely no idea what she was referring to. Tara looked at me with wide-eyed amazement as if to say, "It *is* true!" I was both tickled and amazed by her absolute gullibility. It didn't enter her mind that we had never actually seen any mermaids lounging around the lake, that Eli could not swim and would have a hard time stealing away to hide necklaces in the woods, that ducks do not talk, and so on. Her thinking was a perfect illustration of what Jean Piaget describes as preoperational or intuitive thinking—long on magic and short on logic. It's analogous to how young children never think about how Santa's girth couldn't really fit down the chimney, or if it takes Santa ten minutes to visit each house and there are 700 million households in the world . . .

Over the next week, there were numerous references to the necklace. One day when she couldn't find it, she worried. "Uh-oh. Maybe the mermaids came to steal it back." After we returned home, two hundred miles away, she shared with the babysitter her concern that the duck might come and take back the necklace. The story lived on vividly in her mind, and the logical inconsistencies just didn't exist.

It's this mode of story consciousness that I was trying to support during Tara and Eli's early childhood. Stories and dreams had the same weight as everyday life, the same valence for Tara at this point in her life. It's true for all children. It's hard for us to imagine this state of mind. Think about the last time you had a nightmare, how you woke up with the fear lying heavily on you like a lead apron. It felt so real that it was hard to shake the images. That's how children experience dreams and stories all the time. Or think of it like baking a marble cake. The everyday events are the vanilla cake batter into which the chocolaty stories and dreams get folded. When memory bakes the cake, it's all the same texture—you can't tell the difference between the two different swirls of cake.

Some may consider stories like these to be deceitful trickery, leading children astray and confusing them about the nature of reality, so let me share some of my motives. I like the idea of having children live into stories because it prepares them to imagine how life can be, and then encourages them to make it so. In this case, I told the Mermaids and the Necklace story and then actualized it by having a tangible necklace appear. As Mary Catherine Bateson suggests in her book *Composing a Life*, the autobiographical experience is like the artist's experience of painting a picture or the writer's process of crafting a story. We each create a story of our life and then shape events to fulfill the story. One's biography is a combination of real events and fanciful creation. In part, we create a story of who we want to be and then find ways into situations to make the story come true.

One of my objectives at this stage of Tara's childhood was to give her a sense that she could compose her own story and make it real. I also wanted her to *live* stories that transformed her into other beings and engaged her in exploring the landscape. And I wanted stories to prod her to use the maps in her head, to encourage her to find her way in the world.

Dreams, too, can be a source of knowledge and power. A friend of mine recounted that one of the most significant insights in therapy for her came when she said, "I just can't decide which is more real, my everyday life or my dream life," and her therapist responded, "Well, both, of course." I have taken pains not to set up dreams and stories in opposition to "reality." That's because I believe there's as substantial a "realness" in dreams and stories as in waking experience. Certainly everyday experience is more concrete and tangible. If you're hit on the head with a rock when awake, it usually hurts more than being hit on the head by a dream—but not always. By revealing the "dream" to Tara as the source of information, I suggested that dreams can be real, and this categorical truth was more important to me than the "truth" that I didn't really have that dream. Moreover, I wanted to cultivate the notion that following your dream is a useful and valuable thing to do. That's the deeper truth.

Tara graduated from Bennington College in June 2009. For her senior project she wrote and produced an original play: a family melodrama about a failed relationship, a daughter who runs away, a father who communes with the trees. There was even a tree spirit, whose voice emanates out of the darkness. (Remember that angels used to live among us but now they live in trees.) The play grew from an image that Tara developed into a script. A few elements were autobiographical, but many emerged from an improvisational process Tara facilitated with the cast. She recruited ten actors and dancers, implemented a rehearsal schedule, and directed the play. She did original choreography, designed costumes, and composed appropriate mood music. It was set outdoors in a pine grove at night, which required challenging set design and lighting. Along the way there were a multitude of problems to solve—how to deal with actors griping about their too-busy lives, how to get electricity out into the woods, how to get the tree spirit's voice to emanate from the dark treetops, how to move the audience to different parts of the set.

Tara's creation and production of this play is a good example of life as a composable story. The play started as an image—a glimpse of a dream, a fragment of a story—and through the endeavors just described was incrementally translated into reality. And it all unfolded in the woods, at night—a place Tara had become comfortable with in childhood.

I contend that Tara's playwriting and producing capacities were roughed in during our early storytelling experiences. When she was about eight, Tara described what happened when she listened to one of my stories. "When you started to tell the story, I saw pictures in my head, and then when you kept on, I went into Dreamland as you told the rest of the story and watched it happen." By telling stories, and then extending and inhabiting them as we did with the Mermaids and the Necklace story, I was preparing her to see the productive relationship between an imagined world and the everyday, shapable "real" world.

Thoreau once said, "If one advances confidently in the direction of one's dreams, and endeavors to live the life which one has imagined, one will meet with a success unexpected in common hours." When Tara went into the Mossy Woods and found the necklace, she was living the life once imagined.

How does the kind of storytelling I practiced—featuring magical realism and outdoor settings—nurture adult capacities? Being able to enter into one's imagination fully, or to recall dreams and use them to guide your life, are faculties we often try to recapture as adults. The novelist struggles to find the doorway in her mind that allows her to enter into the story she's creating. A study by British developmental psychologists shows the link between complex imagined fantasy worlds in childhood and creative fiction. C. S. Lewis's Narnia was originally a fantasy world created by the author and his brother during childhood outdoor play. Willa Cather's experience in the childhood make-believe village of Sandy Point, created by Willa and her friends, inspired much of her later writing.

There are numerous stories of scientists whose dreams led to scientific breakthroughs: August Kekulé's dream of a snake biting its own tail led to his discovery of the carbon ring structure of the benzene molecule. It works for visual artists too. Jasper Johns painted for several years without finding recognition and success. In 1954, he was inspired by a dream to paint a large American flag, and his series of flag paintings established him as a major artist.

These and other recent findings confirm my sense that it was one of the best inventions as a parent to compose stories out of the strands of our life outdoors. As adults, we rarely take the time to weave magic into our lives, and the opportunity for parents and teachers to reach children in this way is limited to the years of early childhood. By the time they are seven years old, some of the facility of imagining will start to fade as logical thinking ascends. My aim in crafting stories set in woodland, waterland, and dreamland was to support fluid movement between two parallel dimensions. I wanted my children to move from everyday experience into story and dream and back again as easily as moving from one room to another, and to feel as comfortable out in the evening mist as cuddled up on the couch inside.

The story worlds we created wove together home and nature, light and dark. Anticipating the next stage, the story world also blazed pathways from the early childhood meadow into the middle childhood forest, pathways the child will start to follow on his own.

Together in Dreamland
Bridging the Sadness of Separation

Think back to your first experiences of aloneness. Following the dog into the woods at the edge of your yard, then turning around and not being able to see your house. Feeling that surge of panic and tears: Will I be able to find my way home? Or, in the supermarket, you look up and realize the hand you just grabbed does not belong to one of your parents. "Where's Mommy?!" you wail, and she quickly appears around the corner from her quick jaunt to the pet food aisle. Maybe it was the first day of kindergarten. You've just hung up your sweatshirt and taken your place in the circle on the rug, and your red-haired teacher seems really nice and smiley. But when you turn around, you see your mother waving and sliding quietly out the door. You thought she was going to be there for the whole morning! The realization that *she's leaving* sweeps over you like a bad dream, and you try not to cry even though you feel abandoned. It's a long three hours.

These first memories of being separated from parents, especially from mother, are intimations of the transition from early childhood to middle childhood. To move from feeling safe in the family to feeling safe in the big world out there, children have to gain skills of pathfinding, comforting themselves, and depending on their wits. An emotional foundation of dealing with aloneness needs to be laid. It can be done unintentionally, without care for the inner emotional life of the child, or thoughtfully, with an eye toward developing the child's inner resourcefulness.

My children embarked on this journey later in the summer of the Mermaids and the Necklace stories. It was mid-August and we had returned home from the family vacation in Maine. The next event of the summer was Wendy's departure on an eleven-day women's canoe trip in Ontario. She would not be reachable by phone most of that time and had never been gone for more than two nights at a stretch since Tara's birth. I anticipated being a single parent for this long period with mixed excitement and trepidation. The children (again, Tara was five that summer and Eli three) were feeling shaky. They were used to spending big chunks of time with me alone, but they sensed that this was going to be quite different. It would be an emotional challenge for everyone.

As Wendy's departure approached, the children become increasingly fragile. "Don't go canoeing, Mommy. Don't go!" they pleaded and sobbed. But she stuck to her plan, and I'll describe what happened in the present tense, largely as it was recorded in my journal.

Follow the Stream

Wendy leaves in the evening and that first night is unsettled. Tara cries herself to sleep and has a fitful night. Eli wakes up frequently. We all start the next day feeling lonely and like motherless children. I am not prepared for how melancholy I feel and am a bit daunted by my sense that I have to hold all the emotional pieces together for both children. While Eli seems fairly cheery during the day, Tara is having a harder time. Before lunchtime she dissolves into a puddle of tears. "I miss Mommy. I want Mommy to come home!" It takes a while for her "to get all the crying out," as she puts it.

That afternoon I realize I need to do something to raise our spirits. Based on my recent success with stories about dreams, I devise a plan. I take both children out to the hammock to be close. We bring a couple of pillows and a blanket, and settle into the dappled shade under the apple trees. I put an arm around each of them and tell a story, mostly for Tara's benefit.

Once there was a little girl whose mother was going away for a long trip. The little girl was staying home with her brother and her father. They were planning lots of special things, but the little girl was afraid that she was going to miss her mother terribly. Before she left, she cried and cried. "Please don't go away, Mommy. I'm going to miss you."

The day before she left, the mother sat down with the little girl. She said, "I know you're going to miss me and I'm going to miss you too. We'll both feel sad. But I have an idea. When you go to sleep at night, you'll go into Dreamland. And when I go to sleep, I'll go into Dreamland too. And even though I will be very far away in Canada, all the streams flow together to connect all the parts of Dreamland. When you go into Dreamland, find a stream and follow it. And when I go into Dreamland, I'll find a stream and follow it, and we will meet where the streams flow together. We'll stay together in Dreamland for a while and then we'll hug each other goodbye and follow our streams back to our own beds."

That night the girl went to sleep and went into Dreamland, and when she got there she found a beautiful, crystal-clear stream. It rippled gently and flowed through a mossy forest. She walked and walked until she came to a place where another stream joined, and together they flowed over smooth, gently sloping rocks to form lots of little carved pools. She looked into the bottom of one of the pools and found some sparkling, polished stones. She reached in to pick them up and just then noticed her mother's reflection in the surface of the pool.

She looked up, and there was her mother standing next to her! They collected stones, waded in the cool water, and lay down in the moss next to the stream. When it was time to go, they gave each other big hugs and kisses, then the little girl walked back along the stream to her bed and her mother walked back the other way. When the girl woke up the next morning, she felt happy because she had visited her mother in Dreamland.

I pause for a moment to make it clear that the story is finished. "So, Tara, maybe *you* can try to visit Mommy tonight, like the little girl in the story." She looks both intrigued and unsure about this idea, but willing to try. When I put her to bed that night, I remind her about the story and she nods in acknowledgment.

When I ask her at breakfast if she visited Mommy last night, she immediately provides the following description. (The following excerpts are quoted directly from my journal.)

AUGUST 19, 1991   I was in Dreamland. I followed the little stream and I met Mommy and we swam in the pools. She went back to where she was and I went with her. The only part of land was a beach, and there was water everywhere. She found a place where someone had been digging, and we found a box with necklaces and pearls. I get to keep them, but I can't tell anyone or my wishes won't come true. I stayed with her a little while and then I came back home.

I nod acceptingly and tell her I'm pleased that she got to visit Mommy, but internally I am giddily amazed that the scheme actually worked. On the other hand, perhaps she's just making up a quick story on the spot, to take care of me. Or it could have come from the hypnagogic state, that halfway point between waking and dreaming when ideas from waking life morph into dreams. But I am struck by her tone of voice and the straight-ahead way, with no hesitations, in which she describes her dream. The fact that her account contains new elements, for example, that "the only part of land was a beach and there was water everywhere," makes it sound like true dream imagery. Her tone also sounds similar to previous occasions when she has shared dreams.

Wherever Tara's description comes from, her emotional state seems to be different. Later that day she says, "I don't miss Mommy so much because I feel like I'm a part of her and I'm sort of her heart."

The next two mornings, she describes these encounters:

AUGUST 20, 1991   I met Mommy in Dreamland, and there were pools and waterfalls. And you know what? The pools were made not just from water, but also with diamonds. Mommy and I took off our clothes and slid from one pool down the waterfall to another pool, and then down another waterfall and another waterfall.

AUGUST 21, 1991 I met Mommy in Dreamland. We swam through a pool and through a cool flickering stream, and it flowed all the way to Africa and we danced all night. We saw lions and giraffes and I got to ride a giraffe, a baby one. And I rode baby horses and I got a beautiful hat there with roses around it. And then we went back to our places.

By this point, I am becoming a believer. The changing quality of the events in Dreamland that she reports from day to day suggests that she is really having these dreams. Wendy has talked about taking a trip to Africa when Tara is thirteen years old, so it makes sense that this would emerge in the dream. Riding on giraffes and hats with roses, however, are not anything I have ever heard them talk about, and these sound like genuine dream images. This same day, I overhear Tara talking to Jodi, the babysitter, unaware that I am listening. She says, "I miss my Mommy, but I know I can visit her in Dreamland at nighttime." The Dreamland experiences seem to be serving as the emotional bridge that I had hoped for.

I think some of the success of my dream-seeding story lay in its natural-world imagery. The geography of Dreamland had at least two important elements. First, it had recognizable features from Tara's biography. She'd walked along streams with Wendy, had seen streams converge, had experience with streams widening into swimmable pools. Second, the dream drew on deep archetypes, the stuff of myths and fairy tales: the crystal-clear stream in the mossy woods, the glittery stones, the paths coming together, the garden of Eden. Such images are buried deep in our cultural and biological genes. I suspect that the infrastructure of Dreamland as a correlative to the natural world is something we all carry around inside us. Therefore, it made sense to construct the connection to Mommy using an idealized natural-world scaffolding.

Finding Solace in Nature

Two more days pass before I ask about Dreamland again. Tara's been having crying spells each day, and her mood seems to be deteriorating.

She seems as melancholic and sad as the first night. When I ask her if she visited Dreamland last night, she says, "I went to Dreamland to visit Mommy but she wasn't there and I miss her." She starts to cry.

That evening, I am putting her to bed and the sobs begin again. I lose my patience and raise my voice. "Tara, I'm tired of this! Mommy's gone and we all feel sad but we have to get used to it. Look, she'll be back in four days. That's not very long. Now, stop crying."

"Daddy, stop yelling at me! Sadness is like the stripes on my dress. The stripes go in and out. The blue stripes come out and the white stripes go in. The sadness comes inside me and goes outside, back and forth. Now don't you see?"

I feel put in my place and remind myself of the importance of riding with the ebb and flow of the appropriate sadness that she describes.

The next day, when Eli is napping, I take Tara back out to the hammock. I have another story to tell.

Once there was a little girl whose mother was going away on a canoe trip. The girl was sad that her mother was going away, so her mother told her that they could visit each other in Dreamland every night. ("Daddy, you already told me this story," Tara interrupts. "Just wait a minute," I chide and continue.)

The little girl visited her mother in Dreamland, and they had wonderful times together finding treasures and sliding down waterfalls and dancing in Africa. Then one night the little girl went to Dreamland and walked along the stream, and her mother didn't come. She waited and waited, and still she didn't come. She walked back along the stream and went back to her bed, and when she woke up the next day she was very sad.

The next night when the girl went to sleep, she didn't bother to go to Dreamland because she didn't want to feel sadder. That night her mother walked along the stream and waited and waited at the pools, but the little girl never came. The mother went back to where she was sleeping and was upset. She was concerned that something was the matter with the little girl.

The mother talked to all her friends about how upset she was. She wanted to meet the little girl in Dreamland again, but she wasn't sure how to make it happen. The mother and her friends couldn't call on the phone, so they decided to try to send a message to the little girl a different way. They decided they would talk right into the father's mind and get him to tell a story to the little girl to encourage her to visit Dreamland again.

As I finish, Tara's face looks surprised, bemused, and puzzled. Then the realization dawns on her.

"You mean this is the story you were supposed to tell?"

"Yes," I affirm.

"I can hear them whispering to me in my mind right now," she declares. "'Come to see Mommy in Dreamland tonight, Tara. Come to see Mommy.'" She leans over and whispers this last comment in my ear to demonstrate what she is hearing. We decide that Wendy and her friends are trying two different ways to communicate with us to make sure she gets the message. The next morning I inquire about her dreams and she reports quite cheerily.

AUGUST 25, 1991   I walked along the stream and met Mommy, and we came back to the house and it was the strangest thing. You weren't here. We looked all around and we walked down to the frog pond, and you were there with Eli. You were fishing for frogs. You put bugs on and then rolled the line in. (With her hands she gestures putting bugs on hooks and reeling in line.) Then we all came home and Mommy went back. We were all awake during this part; it wasn't a dream.

Later that day Tara is playing with Bun-bun, her stuffed animal. I listen from another room as Tara suggests to Bun-bun they play that she's going away on a canoe trip and Bun-bun has to stay home. As Bun-Bun, she says, "Don't go, Tara, don't go. I'll miss you."

"It's okay," Tara answers soothingly. "Just remember, when you go to sleep you can visit me in Dreamland. Just walk along the stream and I'll meet you."

DURING THE LAST TWO DAYS before Wendy returned, Tara was cheery and high-spirited. She had hit a low point about halfway through, correlating with the times when she wasn't going to Dreamland. After the second story, things became progressively more upbeat. When Wendy came home, Tara would refer to the times they met each other, presuming that Wendy had the same experience but apparently not needing her to confirm this. I had briefed Wendy about Dreamland, and she quickly appreciated the strategy and confirmed Tara's experiences.

Tara's last comment in the final dream account is interesting. "We were all awake during this part, it wasn't a dream." She had said this kind of thing many times before; for example: "Peter Pan came and took me away to Neverland last night. I really flew. It wasn't a dream." When I asked her on that occasion, "If I came up to your room while you were in Neverland, would I see you in bed?" she shook her head *no* quite definitively. Her dream experience had the same realness and the same texture as her waking experience. And she felt no logical need to test out her perception. She didn't ask me whether Eli and I really went fishing for frogs. It happened, she wasn't dreaming, she saw it, it just was.

Similarly, Dreamland created a tangible presence, a keepsake memory of Wendy for Tara that she could hold onto while Wendy was gone, regardless of whether it was "real."

Tara's experiences in Dreamland are, I think, a simple example of the possibilities of lucid dreaming in childhood. Lucid dreaming occurs when we take our conscious volitional thinking into our dream life. Many of us have had the experience of getting to a place in a dream where things get uncomfortable and we say, "This is my dream, and I don't want it to go in this direction." Sometimes we will ourselves to wake up at this point. Some people are even more fortunate and can stay vividly conscious while in the dream, bringing a quality of refreshing exhilaration to the dream experience that is distinctly different from the fuzzy, monochrome quality of conventional dream life.

As I suggested earlier, we sometimes experience this conscious shaping of the dream process in the hypnagogic state, the transition between waking and sleeping. Some fortunate few people are skilled enough to decide what they want to dream before going to sleep; they can take this conscious intent into the full dream state and direct their dreams like a captain piloting a ship. But for most of us, it's catch-as-catch-can.

Tara's access to Dreamland each night, her finding of the stream, suggests some volitional control over her dream content. Somehow she was able to hold on to the suggestion from waking life and bring it into her sleep. Once she found the stream and followed it, the fluid, unexpected quality of dream imagery took over. As the dream starts to wane, she seems to be reporting that she returned home (in the dream of August 25), another conscious or volitional act.

Lucid dreaming doesn't happen for most of us because the pathways between dreaming and waking consciousness have become overgrown. We can't find the way anymore, and, moreover, we don't have the time. But in early childhood, when the worlds are still merged, children can go in and out, like the blue-and-white stripes on Tara's dress. For Tara, dream and story were closely woven together: as reported in the preceding chapter, she once said, "When you started to tell the story, I saw pictures in my head and then when you kept on, I went into Dreamland . . . and watched it happen."

By taking advantage of the easy passage between dream life and waking life in early childhood, it's possible to lay down pathways that won't be completely eradicated by the vines of time. And in showing Tara that she could visit her mother by following the stream in Dreamland, I gave her a tool for finding solace when she was alone.

I think that the child's first experiences of finding her way in Dreamland, or through a story situation, are related to feeling comfortable being out in the world alone. They imaginatively prefigure real experiences that come up a few years later. At age five, Tara went off into the imagined or dreamed forest to follow the stream on her own; soon she and Eli would be exploring real woodlands and waterways.

PART TWO

middle childhood
in the forest

PRELUDE

IN MIDDLE CHILDHOOD, the child's needs change, and parenting roles must evolve in synchrony. Whereas very young children learn to bond with nature within the intimacy of family, at this next stage we see the beginnings of separation between the child and parents, in natural settings and elsewhere. Children at this age are often outdoors with their parents, but they also engage in a lot of independent play outdoors with siblings, friends, pets, or on their own. They spend time making, building, damming, molding, collecting—interacting with the stuff of the natural world.

If early childhood was about discovering empathy, middle childhood is about exploration. It's a time for children to move beyond the family to bond with the earth. They should start to be off on their own, finding their own paths in the forest. And it's important for children at this age to be fully in their bodies. They should be running and jumping on trails through the woods, bodysurfing waves, and pedaling bikes.

Children are biologically programmed to have certain kinds of experiences between ages six and twelve, more or less, and it's our parental responsibility to maximize the likelihood that these things happen. First, we need to make sure that children have opportunities for ecstatic moments in nature, when they feel both fully themselves and fully at one with their surroundings. Second, we need to make sure that they engage in appropriate kinds of physical activity in order to develop, as exercise physiologists would say, a full range of movement diversity in their bodies. And third, we need to discipline ourselves to start letting go—that is, letting them go out of our sight—so that they can develop literal and figurative pathfinding skills.

The provocative idea that children have ecstatic moments that lead to feeling at one with nature was proposed by Edith Cobb, a sociologist and anthropologist, in her book *The Ecology of Imagination in Childhood*. Reviewing the autobiographies of three hundred geniuses (including writers, visual artists, inventors, and scientists), she found an intriguing pattern. Many of her subjects pointed to specific experiences in nature during middle childhood that had an indelible effect on their lives.

> There is a special period in middle age of childhood, approximately from five or six to eleven or twelve, between the strivings of animal infancy and the storms of adolescence—when the natural world is experienced in some highly evocative way, producing in the child a sense of some profound continuity with natural processes. . . .
>
> It is principally to this middle-age range in their early life that these writers say they return in memory in order to renew the power and impulse to create at its very source, a source which they describe as the experience of emerging not only into the light of consciousness but into a living sense of a dynamic relationship with the outer world. In these memories the child appears to experience a sense of discontinuity, an awareness of his own unique separateness and identity, and also a continuity, a renewal of relationship with nature as process.

Many artists, in particular, point to experiences in nature during middle childhood that shaped their creativity and their relationship to the natural and wider worlds. In a story from *The Portrait of the Artist as a Young Dog*, Dylan Thomas brilliantly recollects a play experience as a boy fully alive in his body and in nature while playing "Indians" with his friend:

> Down the thick dingle Jack and I ran shouting, scalping the brambles with our thin stick-hatchets, dancing, hallooing. We skidded to a stop and prowled on the bushy banks of the stream. . . . We crawled and rat-tatted through the bushes, hid, at a whistled signal in the deep grass, and crouched there, waiting for the crack of a twig or the secret breaking of boughs.
>
> On my haunches, eager and alone, casting an ebony shadow, with the Gorsehill jungle swarming, the violent, impossible birds and fishes leaping, hidden under four-stemmed flowers the height of horses, in the early evening in a dingle near Carmarthen, my friend Jack Williams invisibly near me, I felt all my young body like an excited animal surrounding me, the torn knees bent, the bumping heart, the long heat and depth between the legs, the sweat prickling in the hands, the tunnels down to the eardrums, the little balls of dirt between the toes, the eyes in the sockets, the tucked-up voice, the blood racing, the memory around and within, flying, jumping, swimming, and waiting to pounce. There, playing Indians in the evening, I was aware of myself in the exact middle of a living story, and my body was my adventure and my name. I sprang with excitement and scrambled up through the scratching brambles again.

This is where the child at age nine or ten wants and needs to be: "in the exact middle of a living story," in which his body is his adventure and his name. The boy here feels completely himself and completely immersed in the natural world—"the Gorsehill jungle swarming." At such moments children feel most fully alive, and they experience the kind of bonding that makes them love the earth and want to protect it. If we can provide children with safe, unstructured nature play—at home, in recreation programs, at summer camp, in after-school programs—then we increase the likelihood of such euphoric moments, which create a repository of inner hopefulness and optimism.

Such experiences are formative not just for geniuses and writers but for anyone. A study of religious experiences in childhood by British psy-

chologist Edward Robinson turned up many examples of transforma-
tional nature experiences from middle childhood. Gazing out of her open
window one early morning before anyone was awake, a woman in her
forties recalls a euphoric moment when she was about six years old:

> The morning sunlight shimmered on the leaves of the trees and on the
> rippling surface of the river. The scene was very beautiful, and quite
> suddenly I felt myself on the verge of a great revelation. It was as if I
> had stumbled unwittingly on a place where I was not expected, and
> was about to be initiated into some wonderful mystery, something of
> indescribable significance.
>
> For the brief seconds while it lasted, I had known that in some
> strange way I, the essential "me," was a part of the trees, of the sun-
> shine, and the river, that we all belonged to some great unity. I was
> left filled with exhilaration and exultation of spirit. This is one of the
> most memorable experiences of my life, of a quite different quality
> and greater intensity than the sudden lift of the spirit one may often
> feel when confronted with beauty in Nature.

Illustrating Edith Cobb's notion of "unique separateness" and "continuity with nature," the woman at the window describes "the essential
me" uniting with the trees, the sunshine, and the river. I contend that
discovering this sense of deep connectedness, of being saturated with nature while yet unique and separate, is one of the core gifts of middle
childhood. Sensing continuity deepens the child's empathic relationship
with the natural world, and being aware of separateness provides a sense
of agency, of being able to take responsible action. The productive uniting of these two experiences, of continuity and separateness, can lead to
a lifelong commitment to protection. As parents, we can't make these
kinds of experiences happen, but we can set the stage for them, as I tried
to do with my children.

The Dylan Thomas passage also speaks to the needs of the young
body in middle childhood, in describing how the boys clamber down the
brambly banks of a stream. Scrambling about in nature promotes the full
range of movement diversity called for at this stage of life, but regret-

tably, most children these days aren't doing enough of it. Sedentary electronic recreation and intensive youth sports have curtailed or changed the ways in which our children move and have affected their physical development. In a 1988 article in the *New York Times*, exercise physiologist Peter Egoscue expresses his concerns about young children who take part in demanding, fast-paced youth sports programs:

> Almost every day, I see the victims of this hectic pace and drive for productivity in my sports injury and exercise therapy clinic. Kids come in bandaged and braced, halt and hurting, like 50-year-olds. Many of these young athletes regard their bad knees, wrenched ankles, and sore shoulders as confirmation that they are playing like the pros. . . . Our kids are getting hurt, not by the games they play or by random mishaps, but by living a sedentary and wildly premature lifestyle.
>
> Youth has a purpose. From a musculoskeletal standpoint, the years between birth and the early twenties are important for building a solid foundation that ensures muscles and joints will operate properly for the rest of life. This happens only one way: unstructured, spontaneous movement. As children, we are programmed by nature to be little whirling dervishes. Crawling, rolling over, walking, running, skipping, throwing, and the like are all intended to form vital physical functions. Moreover, healthy development of the brain stem is directly linked to movement, starting in a mother's womb and continuing for at least the first ten years of life.

Egoscue is advocating for a full range of movement diversity through unstructured spontaneous movement. This happens naturally during free play in nature. Instead, children's opportunities for vigorous free play tend to be limited, and their bodies are sedentary much of the time. Kids don't walk anymore—they ride everywhere, and much of their recreation is finger-based. And the exercise they do get isn't always suitable. Egoscue maintains, "Children and their parents are active and hard working, but in most cases 100 percent of the work is done with about 20 to 30 percent of their musculoskeletal functions." As a result, much of the body's natural physical repertoire atrophies. When children then get involved in youth sports, their bodies aren't fully conditioned, and the demands of the sport aren't appropriate to their physiology. In this scenario injuries can occur that may cause chronic pain for the rest of their lives.

One wonders whether recent increases in learning disabilities and attention deficit disorder can be attributed at least partly to motion starvation. Look at the daily lives of too many children and adolescents—sitting in chairs in school for hours on end, hanging out at malls, more sitting on couches or in front of screens, yet more sitting in cars. Egoscue's prescription? "Instead of Ritalin, Prozac, or knee braces, I'd like to see parents prescribing playgrounds, open fields, and tall trees for climbing. . . . Teenagers and younger children need periods of intense, unstructured play without any purpose other than having a good time." In fact, recent research done at the Human Environment Research Laboratory at the University of Illinois found that play in green outdoor spaces relieves symptoms of attention deficit disorder, while indoor electronic recreation increases these same symptoms. Some doctors are even starting to prescribe outdoor play as part of treatment plans.

We can see in the Dylan Thomas description a perfect portrait of children developing movement diversity. The boys scalp brambles, dance, halloo, skid, prowl, crawl, hide, crouch, pounce, and scramble their way to musculoskeletal health—and no bored parents have to stand around watching on the sidelines

On the subject of letting go, here's a good illustration from the urban wilderness. New York writer Lenore Skenazy (who has since started a website called Free Range Kids) has a son who, at age nine, wanted to have a bit more freedom of motion in Manhattan. They agreed that, as an experiment, she would drop him off at Bloomingdale's and he'd have to find his way home: making his way from Bloomingdale's to the nearby subway station, riding the subway six stops, then taking a crosstown bus to a stop near his apartment. His mom gave him subway and bus fare, but no cell phone.

Skenazy reported on the experiment in her column in the *New York Sun*, writing, "Long story short: my son got home, ecstatic with independence." But the column provoked a firestorm of outrage at what some felt was her negligent, irresponsible, and potentially abusive behavior in providing her child with this bit of scaffolded independence. Well, I'm on her side. Part of bonding with the earth, whether it's in the copse of trees in a subdivision or on city streets, is learning to navigate on your own.

Is there some risk? Certainly. But it's also risky stepping into the shower, where many serious household injuries happen. We don't outlaw showers, though we might put down a sticky mat to reduce the likelihood of slipping. As for navigating a big city, we'd probably ride the route with our child a couple of times before encouraging him to do it alone. Of course, each parent knows best at what age his or her child is ready for this kind of experiment. The point is that the benefit, the child being "ecstatic with independence," is worth some risk. We have to learn to balance benefits versus risks when we make decisions about children starting to explore on their own.

The chapters that follow provide examples of my efforts to scaffold euphoric moments for Tara and Eli, support them in gaining movement diversity and confidence, and then let them go. I've also discussed a few programs around the country that operate from similar intentions.

In "Bare Hands and Bear Dens," the kids and I scramble up ledges, explore caves, get dirty, and meet ravens. Dad explores the psychological terrain of risk-benefit analysis. Then we travel to California to enjoy a day of wild nature play with the Wilderness Youth Project.

In "Burning Brush," Eli goes off to explore the neighborhood and comes back with some hair-raising stories. His metaphoric "playing with fire" leads to some stories about working with fire and the value of learning to master fire in middle childhood.

The theme of magical realism—interweaving real experiences in nature with fantastical elaborations—was introduced in Part One. In "The Emerald Chandelier" Tara and Eli are at a later developmental level, so the stories become more complicated. The settings are more exotic and a bit creepy, and the moments of synchronicity are downright unexplainable.

"Moving in My Heart" recounts my efforts to mediate the pain of divorce for me and the children through getting lost and found in the natural world. We find that closeness to beauty acts as a salve for emotional pain. Chronologically, this essay bridges the middle childhood and adolescence sections of the book.

Bare Hands and Bear Dens
Exploring beyond Home Ground

The beginning of middle childhood correlates with the beginning of first grade. Friends start to become more important, and therefore what your children are doing at other homes starts to shape their outdoor experiences. Are their friends' parents encouraging them to help with farm chores and build hay bale forts, or have they left them upstairs watching television? Other adults start to play a bigger role in children's lives as well. Teachers, after-school program directors, scout troop leaders, and coaches (yes, even as early as first grade) all start to shape children's experiences and values. This is all part of the widening circles of engagement in their lives. Just as children move outward from the home—into the neighborhood or the next subdivision, then into the nearby woods, or beyond Avenue A—they move out into the larger social spheres of school, church, and team. So if we want to cultivate our children's bonds with nature, it's important to choose institutions and other adults who share this commitment.

Wendy and I chose schools for our children based in part on how well the curriculum and philosophy connected children with the natural world. Tara went to the Monadnock Waldorf School in Keene, where her class teacher—with whom the children stay from first through eighth grade—was an outdoorswoman at heart. From regular farm visits in third grade, to backpacking in fourth grade, to caving in sixth grade, to a final class trip sailing in Penobscot Bay in eighth grade, the students received constant exposure to nature. I appreciated how these experiences spiraled outward across the grades—from the school neighborhood to New Hampshire and into more far-flung New England, then across the border to Quebec and finally to the blue horizon, suggesting that they had reached the threshold of the wider world.

Eli's experience at Mountain Shadows School in Dublin, from fifth through eighth grade, was also nature-based. The whole school climbed Mount Monadnock twice a year, the director went barefoot well into October, there was a forts-building domain in the woods behind the school, and farm chores were a part of the daily regimen.

At both schools parents were invited to chaperone class trips as a way to become engaged with the curriculum. Local and state geography is one theme in the fourth-grade Waldorf curriculum: the students in Tara's class explored the neighborhoods around the school on long walks and drew pictorial and panoramic-view maps of the area. Simultaneously Tara's teacher had the students study the plants and animals of New Hampshire. Then each child made a raised relief map of the state in preparation for a three-day hiking trip in the White Mountains.

As a parent chaperone for the outing, I drove Tara and two of her classmates up to the mountains. The valley of the Pemigewasset River narrowed as we approached Franconia Notch, and I started to point out some of the mountains they had learned about when they made their maps. Tara's friend Melinda gazed at the sinuous green peaks, got a faraway look in her eyes, and exclaimed, "I know where we are! Remember where two long low mountains smush in close to the river and then the big mountains are just beyond? We're between those low mountains, and there's Cannon Mountain and the Franconia Range up there."

She gestured with her hands to show the river valley and ridge forms that she had shaped meticulously while making her raised relief map. It was fascinating to watch the mapmaking images stored in her hands and mind snap into resolution with the mountain landscape spread out before us. The inner world and outer world met in this *aha!* moment of well-crafted curricular experience.

The arduous backpacking, group food preparation, inky night walks, autumnal swims, and wind-whipped view from the top of Cannon Mountain bound everyone together in a spirit of hard-won collaboration. The most awesome experience, however, came when we explored a network of boulder caves at the base of the cliffs on the west side of the mountain. For almost an hour the children were like moles on a reconnaissance mission, ferreting out tunnel after tunnel, discovering new passageways and chambers. I encouraged this slightly risky activity because I believe that becoming immersed and submerged in the rocks, soil, moss, and spruce of the real world helps children feel rooted in their native landscapes. On the other side of the mountain, the stone face of the Old Man of the Mountain—an iconic rock formation with a rugged human profile that collapsed in 2003—still gazed out over the jumbly peaks and valleys of northern New Hampshire. In this rock labyrinth, the students were becoming Children of the Mountain.

Spying on Ravens

After seeing the children's enthusiasm for boulder cave exploring, the class teacher and I planned another field trip for the students to Bear Den State Forest, a little-known, off-the-beaten-path piece of protected forest and ledgy outcrops about six or seven miles north of Keene. To prepare for this event, I set aside a day during April school vacation for an outing with Tara and Eli to scout options at that location.

The whole day had the sheen of sun on wet stones. It was the perfect time of year to be there: the bears (if there were any) had left their dens by now, and the blackflies that make forest outings miserable in May were still holed up in their egg cases. The walk in provided lots of puzzles to solve: Whose tracks are these? What made this pile of pinecone pieces? How do we get around this puddle? Can we hop the stones in this stream without getting our feet wet? Are these berries good to eat? Do you think we can find the first blossoms of trailing arbutus? We oohed and aahed at the potholes scoured in a cliffside: How could they have been made when there's no stream nearby?

When we got to the foot of the cliff, where the bear dens are located, I laid out some safety rules, and then they were free to explore. It took no more than a minute for the cries of "Awesome!" to come bubbling up from the crannies and crevices of the talus slope. Though many of the boulder caves were still filled with ice, some tunnels and chambers were explorable. We peered into some that were inky black and too foreboding to enter. Others were roomy and open with craftily constructed stone fireplaces built by previous visitors. A tunnel of thirty feet traveled through a chilly low spot, filled with the refrigerated air of a melting miniglacier. We found porcupine scat in the back of cozy rock nooks. Following tiny footpaths along the face of the cliff, we came to recesses where beech leaves had naturally accumulated and made soft beds big enough for all three of us. We settled in, nibbled on gummy bears (evoking the real black bears out there foraging for grubs), and told silly stories.

Eventually we figured out a route to the top of the cliff, past house-size boulders and rivers of ice to a warm picnic outpost. While Tara napped in the sun, Eli and I explored the cliff face, creeping cautiously along narrow rock ledges until we finally found our way to a flat, vaulted precipice on which to stretch out in the sun. As we lay there, toasting in the warmth, little grunts and squawks percolated into my consciousness and I realized we had animal company of some sort very nearby. We imitatively squawked and heard answering squawks from down below on the face of the cliff. I leaned out over the cliff face, but whatever was squawking was tucked underneath us, just out of sight. By moving to the corner of the cliff and leaning way out, I could see an immense nest full of very large black birds. Nestling ravens!

Eli wanted to see too, and we figured out that if he squirmed his upper body out over the cliff while I held his legs firmly, he could catch a glimpse. We could even look down into their gaping pink mouths, which were as wide as my outstretched hand. Tara joined us and, mastering her own fear of exposure and height, was also able to get a view. The close encounter with these inaccessible creatures made us feel like the recipients of a rare gift.

This family outing had a "just rightness" about it that felt emblematic of developmentally appropriate environmental education. My children and I were united in common purpose to explore the landscapes and mysteries of our extended backyard, our bioregion. We learned natural history, practiced finding our way in the woods, confronted our fears of heights and darkness and enclosed places, took on reasonable physical challenges, and had a magical encounter with wild animals. In the course of our adventures I had the opportunity to describe glacial geology, the food preferences of squirrels and porcupines, the nesting behavior of ravens, the heaviness of cold air, and the medicinal uses of goldthread. We were muddied, scraped, and awed by the natural world as it bound us together in adventure and wonder.

Balancing Risks and Benefits

During Tara and Eli's middle childhood years, I aspired to this kind of outdoor exploring with them. We searched out caves, climbed trees, rock-hopped along shores, built dens in the woods, challenged each other to balance-walk fallen trees over streams, searched out good swimming holes. Two recurrent principles underlay how I structured our adventures.

First, I believed that *it's good for children to explore on their own*. It was my job to teach them to climb safely, to assess risks, to make reasonably sure that there were no significant hazards present, and then to let go. At the bear dens they were often out of my sight, and I'd get nervous, but I worked hard to control my anxiety, knowing that the exploration was worth the risk.

In evaluating what I was prepared to let my children do in the outdoors, I found myself moving away from a mind-set of "risk assessment" to a mind-set of "risk-benefit analysis." In other words, it's important to develop a balanced understanding of both the risks and the benefits of play behavior. All play, including nature play, involves some risk, but that's part of the value: learning how to measure the risk and behave appropriately. The riskiness of play is, to a certain extent, its benefit. Take all risk out of the situation and it's no fun—and not terribly beneficial.

The second principle at work that day at the bear dens was that *exploring leads to educating*. I didn't go into the woods with a curriculum in mind, a predetermined lesson plan about teaching animal habitats or food webs or hibernation. But all those things emerged naturally in the course of our exploration. Too often, traditional environmental education comes at things the other way round, and the educating eclipses the exploring. Children must stay on the trail, not touch things, watch out for the slippery rocks, stay away from the edge, and listen as the adult lectures. Educators and parents fall into the same trap, not realizing that it's the bare-hands experience that creates the relationship that then creates the thirst for knowledge.

The Virtues of Adventure Play

There are, of course, many options for giving children valuable experiences in nature outside the family context: from school trips to summer camps to scouting to more intensive programs such as Outward Bound or youth-oriented outings run by organizations such as the Sierra Club. I won't try to survey them, but only to note that the most successful such programs—in terms of awakening and feeding kids' latent hunger for outdoor exploring—share the principles I've just articulated.

One example is Adventure Playgrounds, created by Carl Theodor Sørensen and implemented throughout the United Kingdom and Europe. Sørensen, a Danish landscape architect, noticed that children preferred to play everywhere but in the playgrounds that he built. In the 1930s he imagined "a junk playground in which children could create and shape, dream and imagine a reality." Why not give children in the city the same chances for free play as those in the country? He created playgrounds full of boards, discarded roofing, and other loose parts that allowed children to shape their own realities. Originally called "junk playgrounds," the name was changed to "adventure playgrounds" when the idea was imported to England after World War II.

Because the programs at these playgrounds involve construction, moving heavy objects, and experimenting with materials, they are staffed by "playworkers," adults whose job it is to provision play but not get too much in the way. This requires them to be perpetually involved in managing risk. Asserting the benefits to children's spirit of free exploratory play, Lady Allen of Hurtwood, an early leader in the Adventure Playgrounds movement, declared, "Better a broken bone than a broken spirit." This saying is displayed cheekily on the staff members' T-shirts at Play Wales, a formal organization of playworkers in Wales.

For parents who need a model of parenting children into nature, I recommend that you search out Nature Mentoring programs. These programs were started by Jon Young, a student of tracking expert Tom Brown Jr. and founder of the Wilderness Awareness School in Seattle, Washington. (Young's recent book, *Coyote's Guide to Connecting with Nature,* is a treasure trove of wisdom and activities for parents and outdoor educators.) Similar programs have proliferated in many states around the country. The nature mentors do a wonderful job of manifesting the two principles I have articulated above: letting children explore on their own within reasonable limits, and understanding that exploring leads to educating.

In October 2006 I spent a day in Santa Barbara with the Wilderness Youth Project, which practices the nature mentoring techniques originally articulated by Young and his colleagues. I had the good fortune to go along on an outing with about a dozen children—black, white, and Hispanic—aged seven to eleven, three leaders, and a handful of parents. I was thrilled to experience their healthy and playful approach to connecting children with nature.

We walked up a trail through Tucker's Grove County Park along a dry wash, a narrow city park surrounded by suburban housing developments on both sides. It was just about a mile up and back, but so much happened along the way. Whereas in so much environmental education the emphasis is on talking about endangered species or food chains or the effects of climate change, here the focus on was on creating opportunities for children to interact with the landscape. Three factors in particular made this outing different from what usually happens when children and adults are in the woods together.

Children had the opportunity to play freely. The youngsters were allowed to climb up the crumbly bank along the trail, or seat-slide down the steep bank to the dry streambed. No admonitions to stay on the trail were heard. When we came upon a fallen oak, kids immediately jumped up to balance-beam-walk along the trunk and the large limbs, then jump off. Instead of hustling them along, the leaders realized that this kind of play was exactly what the children needed to be doing, and they provided the time and structure so each child could engage at his or her level.

When we came upon a child-sized fort, made by a previous group and simulating a wood rat's nest, children spontaneously started to crawl through it. One said, "This is so awesome. I am so not afraid in here. I could live here and do all my projects here." As soon as he was out, he said, "I'm going to do it again," and there was time for that.

Farther on, some of the boys found a little hole in the trail and wondered what it was. They probed it with sticks, then decided to hide some treasures in it, cover it up, and look for it on the way back. An hour later—though it was hard to differentiate this stretch of trail from sections that looked just like it, and no adult reminded them to look—they remembered the spot and were thrilled to unearth an acorn, a marble rock, a bit of clover. What a simple challenge and what an appropriate way to develop observation skills.

A supportive, can-do attitude prevailed, and fear was banished. At one point we had to pass through a gate in a fence. One of the boys wanted to skip the gate and try to climb over the fence, which was topped by a strand of barbed wire. I expected to hear the normal adult responses, "No, you might rip your pants" or "Why don't you just go through the

gate?" or "Let me lift you over" or "Please stop that! It's too dangerous."
Instead, as soon as Kelly, one of the mentors, recognized his intention,
she said, "Great idea to try to climb over, Joshua. Would you like someone to spot you?" Once he was over, she crowed, "Good job! I knew you
could do it." I was impressed that his intention was noticed, validated,
and encouraged. Moreover, she refrained from overinvolvement, providing just enough support to make the process reasonably safe but letting
him solve the problem.

Along the trail, one of the children found an orange ring-necked snake.
Recognizing that it was harmless, Kelly encouraged the child to pick it up
and hold it caringly. Everyone else gathered into a circle to get the opportunity to hold it, as the mentors modeled appropriate ways of holding and
passing the snake. One girl whispered emphatically, "I could *never* hold a
snake!" But as she watched everyone else do it, I could see she was thinking about it. The mentor, sensing an opening, passed it to her and she took
it into her hands with a look of mixed trepidation and wonder on her
face. After she handed it off, Kelly said, "Isn't it great that you were really
scared about holding the snake but you found you could do it? You did
something you didn't think you could do, and it was really cool."

There were many questions and only some answers. When we would
come upon something, a bug or some scat, I'd prepare myself for the boring mini–natural history lecture. "Oh, did you know that's a California
katydid and it lives only in the west-facing coastal chaparral slopes. It
has six legs and three body parts—the head, abdomen and the thorax
and blah, blah, blah." Instead, a mentor might say, "Hmm, I wonder
what that is? Hey, how many legs does it have? Wow, look at those big
eyes—they look kind of greenish to me. What color do they look like to
you? What should we call this bug?" Then later on, during snack time,
a mentor pulled out an insect guide, found the right page, and passed it
to the children who had been looking at the insect. Instead of saying, "I
think it's the California katydid," the mentor said, "Does that bug we
found on the trail look like any of the bugs on this page?" The whole
orientation was to encourage the kids to observe, wonder, see patterns,

and make sense of things. Eventually there were names and concepts, but in a delicate proportion.

On the way back—after a glorious mud fight, splooshing mud with their feet, smearing mud on their bodies—the kids scampered down the trail alone or in pairs. Many were barefoot; some scrambled into the brush to hide and scare the next group on the trail. Kids lagged behind to collect marble rocks or sneak up on others. Nobody was concerned if kids were on their own for a few minutes. Two boys, sneaking along the trail parallel to the main group, froze whenever anyone saw them. They whispered, in clandestine explanation, "We're mysterious Stalking Red Trees."

To wrap up, we sat in a circle in a field riddled with gopher holes, where we had started earlier that afternoon. One of the children said, unprompted, "Three hours isn't enough for these trips. We should do five hours, we should do all day, we should do twenty-four hours. We should build forts and live out here." It was as if the children had dropped into their wild selves and become creatures of the woods, comfortable and at home in their minds, bodies, and native habitats.

The adventures at the bear dens and in Santa Barbara share the same core values. The nature mentors and I believe that wild play is inherently valuable. It develops coordination and self-confidence. It encourages children to explore, observe, and question; it makes them feel fully alive. Going further, I contend that wild play is the crucible in which hope is born, a sense of wonder is crystallized, and the fortitude to deal with the big challenges ahead is forged.

I also share with the nature mentors a common approach to risk-benefit analysis. We are knowledgeable about risks in the landscape—poisonous plants and insects, aggressive animals, slopes unsafe for climbing—and make sure we're choosing activities that have a modest amount of risk, but not too much. When we become overly fearful of a bump or a scrape, we sacrifice the benefits of play.

An analogy to organized sports is useful here. We let our children play soccer despite the risks involved. The benefits of kids getting aerobic exercise, learning teamwork, and developing coordination skills outweigh our concerns about shin splints, cuts and bruises, and the possible broken bone or concussion. A good coach can manage risks but not eliminate them. The same applies to climbing a tree. It's aerobic, it develops coordination skills, it heightens geographic understanding. And, as with playing soccer, there are some risks. Yet despite data suggesting that organized sports are more likely to cause injury than nature play, parents and educators increasingly outlaw tree climbing while supporting soccer.

As parents and educators with a different viewpoint, it's our job to recognize and articulate the benefits of nature play: it contributes to children's health and builds a relationship with the earth. Children need ample time to get their bare hands dirty while exploring bear dens. They will have plenty of time later on to learn about climate change and water shortages. In childhood, they need a big dose of exploring and loving the natural world.

Burning Brush
Playing with Fire

With Tara and Eli, the transition from the backyard, parents-and-children-together experiences of early childhood to the out-and-about, children-exploring-on-their-own stage of middle childhood took several forms.

One transitional form was a game called Lost Children, created by Tara with Eli as willing supplicant, when Tara was about seven and Eli five years old. They'd go just beyond the edge of the yard, down into the nearby trees, and play at taking care of themselves in the woods. It was a combination of Hansel and Gretel and the Boxcar Children. They looked charming as they headed off into the wilds of the backyard with their mini-backpacks, holding each other's hands.

Another game was Sally the Salamander, again designed by Tara. Tara was the Little Girl and Eli was Sally the Salamander, her pet. Eli (who at some point conveniently moved into the role vacated by the imaginary friends and fairy-angels of Tara's early childhood) would compliantly wiggle along the ground when necessary. Tara, of course, couldn't let Eli have all the fun of getting down and dirty; it was a good way for them both to be down on the ground, squirming around, connected with the earth.

As Tara became a big girl of ten or eleven and Eli became eight or nine, their paths diverged, and they started to play with their own gender and age group of friends. They would often be playing at neighbors or in the barn clubhouse down the road, or off on real adventures in the woods. At the time I experienced the same kind of subliminal fear that many parents feel when children head off to play unsupervised, but I worked hard to keep my anxiety in check.

Through a combination of luck and design we lived in a comparatively safe neighborhood. The field next to our house rolls down through mixed woods to hemlock-enshrouded Eliza Adams Gorge below the dam at Howe Reservoir—an accessible playground. In the other direction, a trail leads through a patch of woods to neighbors' houses, a great sledding hill, and a couple of frog ponds. But it wasn't entirely idyllic: back then a house down the road featured rusty pickups and beer-soaked volleyball games. I worried about my kids on bikes when those bleary-eyed guys drove by, way too fast. And when Linda, one of the neighborhood moms, described how a bear trashed her bird feeder on the porch at four in the morning, I worried about what might happen if Tara and the dog encountered it on their way to the reservoir for a swim.

As the children began to venture farther from home, I confronted such dilemmas almost daily. "Should I infect my children with fear, chasten them to be careful, limit bike riding, not let Tara swim unsupervised?" Rather, I'd take a deep breath and do a quick internal risk-benefit analysis. The likelihood of meeting up with a bear was really low. Tara was smart and savvy in the woods. She was a strong swimmer, and she knew if she was on her own she should just swim close to shore. There were benefits in her learning to be independent in the woods and around water. Yes, there was also risk, but probably less than riding in the car to school every morning. I didn't want to sacrifice my children's access to the explorable landscape to the slim possibility of a dangerous situation.

I felt the loss of independent woods play would wound them deeply, and I wasn't willing to take that away.

By the time Eli was seven, I had wrapped up the Night Ride stories, and he soon started creating his own adventures. One December afternoon when Eli was almost nine, I convinced him to help me burn a pile of brush in the back woods. Burning brush is a time-honored New England tradition, an efficient way to get rid of all the broken branches from windstorms or prunings from the apple trees. We had put the brush pile together in the fall as part of cutting firewood; now with snow covering the ground, town regulations allowed burning.

I liked using these opportunities to teach Eli appropriate fire-starting and fire management skills. You create a little hollow under the brush pile where it's nice and dry, crumple up some newspaper, collect dry pine branches, and use them to construct a little log cabin of twigs on top of the paper. Then you douse the construction with half a cup of used turpentine (saved from cleaning paintbrushes), apply a match, and feed the fire with progressively larger twigs until the brush pile starts to catch.

Eli always liked burning. It had a hint of drama and danger about it, and it made him feel grown-up and manly. But after the fire got rolling, one of his friends arrived, and the lure of sledding overcame his interest in the brush fire. Maintaining this fire, and another one I started by myself, occupied my afternoon, and I didn't see Eli for about three hours. He showed up at dusk, unusually abuzz with excitement about his adventures. As he tossed branches onto the fire, he chattered.

Daddy, I found a whole new part of the neighborhood today! I've lived here nine years and it's amazing that I never found this place. I found a bunch of pine trees growing all close together, nine different groups of little pine trees. And we picked one group out and then we climbed all the trees in that group—about seven or eight. You know how at the beginning the trunk is smooth, then there's a bunch of branches coming out and then it's flat again, and then another bunch of branches? We climbed up in one tree, and Joschka and I laid back on the seventh bunch of branches and we rested.

I shut my eyes and I felt like I was going to fall asleep, but I didn't and I was daydreaming about little pathways and walkways through the trees. Like in the *Star Wars* movie where the Ewoks have that little village all up in the trees with suspended bridges connecting the houses together. Or the way squirrels make a pathway from one tree to the next. Then I woke up and thought, "Hey, that's not just a dream. Maybe I can really do that right here." So I tried it.

First you get on to one of the tall trees and then you walk out on one of the long branches and then you hop onto a long branch on another tree. We were up maybe about ten feet off the ground. Then we could zigzag onto another tree and another tree till the fourth tree. I felt like King of the Mountain. Then, ahhhh, I sat down on one of the branches and I slid down bump, bump, bump on each set of branches until I hit the ground. It was so much fun.

Part of me wanted to gasp, "Oh my god, Eli! Do you realize how dangerous that was? You should have a parent help you decide if that's a safe thing to do or not." But he was there, all in one piece, and so I bit my tongue.

We continued to poke the coals and fold in the burnt-off branch ends. The first-quarter moon silvered up the three or four inches of snow on the ground. A bunch of planets appeared. And though it was well below freezing, we worked in our shirtsleeves because of the accumulated warmth of the daylong fire. Eli seemed unusually calm and pensive. He glowed from the exertion and the radiant heat of the coals, but also from the pleasure that comes from true exploration, from trailblazing new terrain. After many minutes of quiet work he continued:

Up until now, I didn't feel comfortable exploring the neighborhood because it felt like I was going to get lost. Now I want to know the whole neighborhood really well so that I can make a perfect map of it. I want to know it just as well as I know all the houses along the road. I'm a good explorer because I really look at all the details, all the little places you can go, all the crannies you can find. I don't just look at it and go, I spend a lot of time on it, make forts and stuff and traps.

As it should be, I thought to myself. This is the kind of outdoor play many of us knew as children—when fanciful dreams were transmuted into real life. When you looked back and realized, "Hey, we really did that!" It's in these moments that children learn that their images of how the world could be can actually shape the world. This is what genuine empowerment is all about, but sadly it's the exception today, and childhoods are impoverished without it. A fellow fifty-year-old dad commented to me around this time:

> When I was young, I'd leave the house in the morning with my dog and we'd be gone all day. I'd catch frogs at the pond, go to the playground, ride my bike all over town, and I'd finally show up back at home eight hours later, muddy and wet and bug-bitten and completely happy. Nowadays, my kids wouldn't know what to do all day out by themselves, and I wouldn't let them go. They've lost the ability to play outdoors.

Haven't you heard some parent speak this way, and doesn't it make you sad? Sad not just in a nostalgic good-old-days way, but because you sense that a child's life without wild play is diminished. The glad animal play of childhood, the complete immersive quality, is one of the elixirs of life and also one of the indispensable proteins that build a sturdy adult soul. Middle childhood offers a window of opportunity to have these experiences, and if a child misses that opportunity, the quality of immersion is less accessible later in life. When, as adults, we sink into a novel or get lost in creative work or tussle with new ideas or improvise on the job, we're using the skills that were roughed in during childhood play. Recalling the powerful moments of childhood, we think of being perched high in the top of a wind-swaying tree, the swooping chase down the alleyway, being tumbled in a wave. Will our children think back as fondly, or as productively, on trading Pokemon cards?

We choose to preserve outdoor play because it feeds the soul, trains the mind, and gives children the kind of drenching good-night's sleep that means they spent the day fully alive. Eli learned something that

December afternoon. He learned that the world is continually unfolding, continually opening up. That when you shake hands with the world, the world shakes back.

And he learned to follow his nose to sniff out new possibilities. A couple of weeks later, we were lying in bed talking about the day, and he said, "When Joschka and I were sledding today, I thought I saw a new hill to sled on. At the end of the flat part, I looked down through the woods and saw this field with clumps of trees, like a glade. I didn't go today because I wanted to save it for another exploration day. It's like saving presents at Christmas. Tomorrow, or the next day, I'll open it up."

Kindling the Flame

In his wonderful essay "A Separate Hearth," Kim Stafford describes his secret place in the woods and the role of fire in finding his new independent self out there in the big world. Describing his boyhood pursuits around eleven or twelve years old, he says,

> In the woods by myself, fire was the heart of it all. In my secret den, or in some refuge off the trail, I would seek out the low shade-killed twigs of a hemlock tree, and the ritual of isolation and sufficiency would begin. I would hold a broken branch to my lips to see how dry it was. I would lay a ring of stones, dug into mineral soil, and arrange perfect sticks one over the other. I would slip out one match from the gleaming steel safe in my pocket. Peel off the paraffin cap from its head with my thumbnail, and shield the hearth with my body from the wind. This was the repeated prelude to my identity. When the match burst open in my cupped hands, and the flame climbed obediently through the precise architecture of my kindling, I had made, again, my own portable world in the world.
>
> Here was my private version of civilization, my separate hearth. . . . My parents' house was a privacy from the street, from the nation, from the rain. But I did not make that house, or find it, or earn it with my own money. It was given to me. My separate hearth had to be invented by me, kindled, sustained, and held secret by my own soul, as a rehearsal for departure.

Advocating that it's important for children to play with fire is like, well, playing with fire. It's verboten. But really, it's part of training your children to be safe and responsible in the woods, and responsible for their own lives in a larger sense. Fire safety is something they need to learn, and it's appropriate to model and start to teach fire building when children are in middle childhood. The challenge of letting go as a parent applies here as well. Just as we need to become comfortable with children being on their own, we need to know that they can handle themselves safely around fire.

Eli, like many boys around age nine and ten, was fascinated with making fires. I'd find little piles of matches, scorched twigs, and fire scars on the concrete floor of the barn or in the driveway. These were almost acceptable places for him to practice fire building, but the secretive, un-controlled quality of the behavior made me nervous. In the spirit of har-nessing this energy, I spent the better part of a day building a fire ring in the backyard, out between the garden and the compost pile. I wrestled big rocks from old stone walls and rock piles in the woods, then wedged them carefully so they wouldn't wobble if you stood on them. It was about four feet across. The rule was that fires were to be built here and only here—no exceptions.

I then provided Eli with his own little fire kit, a repurposed red plastic toolbox, provisioned with flint and steel, some tinder, matches, a lighter, and candles. He got particularly good at getting fires going in the rain, and I came to depend on him when I needed to get brush fires going in damp weather. One autumn night he went out to the fire pit after din-ner and returned a couple of hours later. "It was so beautiful out there," he reported. "Just the darkness, the stars, and the fire. I thought I'd be scared and lonely out there all by myself, but it was really cozy. It was almost as if the fire was my friend."

Like Tara's friendship with the moon. Isn't this what we want, this sense of friendship between the physical world and our children? It's so easy to take all the risk and solitude out of our children's lives—don't play with matches, don't go out there alone, no you can't use your pocketknife unless you're with an adult. Instead, we have to support these independent forays, this building of friendship with fire and the dark night. The hand-built fire, like the fort in the woods, is a vehicle of individuation. Both help children become independent selves, become their own parents.

Fire and the Tribe

A generative relationship with fire and independence is cultivated at the Oyase Community School, a wilderness education program located on the banks of the West River in Dummerston, Vermont. A once-a-week program for children six to fifteen years old and their parents, Oyase comes out of the same mind-set as the Wilderness Youth Project in Santa Barbara, described in the preceding chapter. Its leaders are committed to the kind of nature play and development of wilderness skills set forth in Jon Young's *Coyote's Guide.* Led by nature mentors, the children spend one day a week exploring, tracking, building shelters, learning wilderness skills, eating edible plants, storytelling, and making fires using a variety of modern and primitive skills.

In May 2009 I spent an about-to-rain day with thirty-five Oyase children, parents, and mentors. The children and parents had been out in the elements, rain or shine, every Thursday since the previous October. Many families have been committed to Oyase for years, and it was apparent that their children were comfortable and knowledgeable in the woods.

WE ARRIVE AT SOME OLD FARM SHEDS in a field by the river, and everyone tramps up through hemlocks and a sprawly meadow to a big fire circle nestled among the old white pines. After listening to a few poems read aloud, practicing a bit of tai chi under the pines, and making some plans for the day, the children split up into three clans (Beeches, six to eight years old; Hemlocks, eight to twelve years old; and White Pines, twelve to fifteen years old) and head to their home sites, spread throughout the 120 acres of forest.

I tag along with the Hemlocks. Liz, their mentor, greets them and with little instruction dispatches them to their "sit spots," a well-honed tradition. Each child has chosen a special spot, usually isolated and not in view of any other child or adult, and spends fifteen to twenty minutes just sitting, listening to woodpeckers, sensing the cold front moving in, attending to the fresh fragrance of balsam. Children are encouraged to do this practice every day at home as well. Konstantinos, a parent and assistant mentor, says that some of the Hemlocks have been doing this for twelve hundred days in a row—more than three years, through cold snap and heat wave. It's refreshing to see children who feel completely settled in quiet contemplation—and adults who are comfortable with children being alone and unsupervised in the woods.

Regathered at the home site, the Hemlocks lay out their plans for the day. First, everyone has to participate in the ritual of fire building. The ultimate skill is to make fire using a bow drill, a tool each of them has made that generates an ember for starting a fire. This is no mean feat, and it often takes months to refine the skill. The children fluidly subdivide into work groups. One group disperses to collect firewood. They know about seeking dead and dry wood and sorting it into piles of different sizes. Wood collected, this group constructs a tepee of tiny dry twigs where the fire will start.

Another group makes tinder from birch bark. Ten-year-old Sophie, aka Gray Fox, is the tinder expert. She gives me a piece of white birch bark and shows me how to peel off layer after layer of the thinnest, onionskin-like sheets of inner bark. Then the sheets are rubbed together vigorously to fray them into a roundish bundle of tinder.

A third group is dispatched to travel back to the main campfire, about a half mile away, to bring back fire in case the bow drill technique doesn't work. They collect a dried-out birch polypore (a woody fungus specific to white birches) to bring with them. It's called a tinder conk. When placed into the fire, it will start to burn. Its unique attribute is that you can get half of it smoldering—its dense fibers will burn for as long as a couple of hours—yet carry it by its other end. Transportable fire! Think about this scenario from a typical public school liability perspective: young boys walking with fire, one of them barefoot, unsupervised in the wild woods.

It's sobering to realize that when children are well trained and trusted, they can handle fire, and themselves, appropriately in the woods.

A final group works with the bow drills. The tool comprises a tiny bow strung loosely with a cord that is wrapped around an upright stick, and a board with a small pit gouged out, to provide footing for the stick. Next to the small pit is a notch in the side of the board that collects sawdust. As the bow is oscillated back and forth at furious speed, the bottom of the stick spins in the pit in the board and generates sawdust and heat. When enough sawdust has been produced and enough sustained heat built up, the little ball of sawdust (now called a coal) will start to smolder. The fire builder introduces the smoldering coal to the birch bark tinder bundle, and blows on the coal to make it glow. If all goes well, the tinder bundle bursts into flame, the fire builder slides it into the twig tepee, and *voila:* fire!

This morning, the fire carriers with the tinder conk get back before the bow drill operators are successful, so they start the fire that way. The whole process happens fluidly, with little adult intervention. The children do a little puffing until the tepee bursts into flame, then they add larger sticks. They are experts with fire. In the meantime, I watch one girl work with Konstantinos for more than an hour trying to generate a coal with a bow drill—a testimony to her physical endurance and commitment.

Right as the fire gets started, it begins to drizzle. The remarkable thing is that no one really minds, or at least no one says, "Oh no, it's raining." The children move their packs into the branch-and-tarp shelter, and some slip on rain jackets, but everyone keeps on with their business. These children are completely at home in the woods, rain or shine.

And they are completely at home with fire. It's clear that these children have made fire their friend. They know how to coax it out of natural materials with their refined knowledge and skills. They know how to handle it carefully, use it as a life-sustaining force, and extinguish the fires they build safely and completely. It is just one of a pantheon of skills—finding your way in the woods, developing a sense of direction, learning to sleep on the ground, deciphering the stories in tracks, finding the quiet place within, knowing which berries are good to eat—that children are biologically programmed to want to learn during middle childhood.

Our knee-jerk reaction to coddle and protect our children at all costs is unproductive. Instead, we need to recognize children's desire to find their own way, have their own adventures, and kindle their own flames, as signs of their necessary independence, and give them the tools that enable their selves to unfold.

The Emerald Chandelier
Magic Realism Revisited

Once upon a time, a long time ago, a story began. Following a jetty out into Long Island Sound, my daughter and I walked and tossed stones. "This one's smoky quartz. See the flecks of mica in this one? When I was your age I collected mica on long lonely walks, a few beaches over to the west. These crystals, black and shiny, they're tourmaline." Tara said something about a princess walking this shimmery path. And so it began. A story about a prince and a princess, an evil dragon, and his quest to complete an emerald chandelier that would give him power over all the inhabitants of all the lands. A story of hundreds of chapters, told over thousands of miles. The crystals, minerals, flora, and fauna of New England glinted and pranced throughout the tellings.

The Quartz and Mica stories, as the kids referred to them, started when Tara was about eight and Eli about six years old. Although it was never stated explicitly, Tara was Quartz, the princess; Eli was Mica, the prince; I was Granite, the king; and Wendy was Silver, the queen.

Throughout their middle childhood years, I told episodes of the story
a couple of times a month, and more frequently during vacation. On
couches in the woodstove warmth of home, north of Monadnock; on
top of the dune cliff in Wellfleet on Cape Cod; in the cove-facing shelter
on Swan's Island, Maine; and one winter in a beachside palapa on the
Yucatan coast of Mexico, the story was a constant thread of family life.

Quartz and Mica were, of course, heroic figures. One of the big ideas
was for the children to see themselves on a grand quest, going on adventures, solving unsolvable problems, collaborating with each other. Just as
in the Night Ride stories with Eli, the Mermaids and the Necklace story
with Tara, and lots of other shorter tales, another big idea was to teach
the natural history of New England between the lines. The storytelling
persisted regularly until they both started to move through adolescence
around thirteen or fourteen.

It didn't completely end, though. Once a year or so, through the high
school years, I'd submit. After one long lapse between chapters, when
Tara was sixteen, I remember beginning to tell the story and watching as
adolescent impatience faded from her face, as her expression shed years,
her body curled back to cozy eleven, and she sank into story mode. I
think there are still chapters to be told. . . .

But let's go back to the middle of the story. In Mexico, on a winter
vacation with another family, we were in the thick of it. Tara, age eleven,
and Eli, age eight, were at the peak of story consciousness, and when I
told the story, everything else stopped. No bickering, no fidgeting, just
that dreamy pictures-in-the-mind's-eye look on their faces. The wild and
windy Yucatan coast was an appropriately eerie place for storytelling.

We were huddled together under mosquito netting in a stone and shell
palapa on the beach, south of the Mayan ruins of Tulum. Outside, the
enormous land crabs were getting ready to scuttle along the paths in the
dark of night. Inside, we lit the kerosene lamps at twilight, knowing that
the generator providing evening electricity wouldn't go on for another
half hour, also signaling the serving of dinner. Just enough time for another episode of Quartz and Mica.

Where were we in the story at this point? Well, the dragon had completed the chandelier and, as a result, he was able to shape-shift any creature into any form he wanted. His goal, of course, was evil hegemony, dark control over the kingdom of Cheshire and all the adjacent lands. In no time, he had created a force of wolves, raccoons, ponies with red eyes, and soldiers who willingly did his bidding. Quartz and Mica were the only ones who could prevent his rise to ultimate power, but at the moment, they were in hiding. When the dragon's troops ransacked their village, they had managed to escape to the land of the gnomes, who inhabited a world of excavated tunnels and caves hidden in the coastal dunes five days' travel from the dragon's castle. But then our heroes heard that Tourmaline, their cousin, had been captured, and the dragon planned to shape-shift him into a mindless simpleton traitor if Quartz and Mica refused to surrender themselves. They had been summoned to appear within two days.

There was no way that Quartz and Mica could make it back to the dragon's castle by sunset, two days from now. But they couldn't bear the thought of slate-haired, clever Tourmaline as a dragon's peon. They feared that glazed look in his eyes, the dribble of drool from the side of his mouth, that so many of the shape-shifted exhibited.

Frosten, their gnome host, still young at 180 years, was eager to help.

"Yer welcome to take a coupla our Welsh ponies. They're not the mean 'uns the dragon's snagged. Nice and gentle, but fast as a January squall off the bay."

But Quartz had already done the calculations in her head. Even if they rode all through the night, tied to the saddles so they wouldn't fall off if they fell asleep, it would still take the better part of three days.

"That's generous of you, Frosten, but it won't do. As fast as they are, we still won't make it in time. And the dragon waits for no one."

Mica, brooding in the corner, cleared his throat and offered, "Do you remember, almost a decade ago, when we still lived in the castle, and the squire wanted to fill the marsh out beyond the south ramparts, to plant new fields for barley and oats? Tourmaline objected because in the far corner, out of sight of the village, there was a stand of skeletal trees. High in the dead branches, in their stick nests, herons nested. It was a rookery.

"We intervened on behalf of the herons. When the squire wouldn't believe us, we convinced the herons to lend us one of the nestlings. We brought it to the courtyard, all gangly and gray, not blue yet at all, and the squire begrudgingly agreed to look elsewhere for. . . ."

"Mica, you're wasting time with your dreamy memories," interrupted Quartz impatiently. "We've got to figure out what we're going to do!"

"That's what I'm doing!" Mica snapped back. "There's a rookery in the marsh at the edge of the dunes here—where the cobble beach makes the stream pond up. I noticed a half dozen nests in there when I was collecting cranberries the other day. The herons offered to return our favor back then. Blue herons are one big extended family. No harm in asking."

The landscapes in the story evoked many places the children knew. The dunes of the gnomes' world are from the Province Lands at the tip of Cape Cod. We had a favorite family walk to "the perfect dune" where we would dune-swim and play king of the mountain. The cobble beach that made the stream pond up was from Swan's Island, where we'd been the previous summer. I hadn't, at this point, been to a heron rookery with them, but I was visualizing one in Ball Basin in Stoddard, New Hampshire. And they both probably remembered my real story of raising an immature blue heron when I was a New Hampshire Audubon naturalist.

Relationship-wise, Tara often lorded it over Eli, thinking she always knew what was best, so giving Mica the role of solving the problem was my attempt to rebalance the power dynamic. But this is much more analytic than what was happening in the moment. I was putting this all together as the telling unfolded.

And so, Frosten canoed them out to the rookery, and he and Mica climbed up to have an audience with the blue heron.

Mica beseeched, "Many thanks, blue heron, for welcoming us into your home. I speak with haste because one of my family is in danger, just like many in your family were threatened some years ago. The dragon's evil spreads across the land and he is about to claim my cousin's soul unless we, my sister and I, can intercede. Has the tale of the herons of Cheshire flown this far—how three young people saved the marsh where herons nested?"

Was that a tear in the heron's eye, Mica wondered to himself? For as he told his story, he noticed the heron tilt its head to the left, and a drop of water dribbled across the bird's bill, tumbled off, just missed the edge of the nest, and plummeted downward.

"Hurry up," Quartz yelled from below. "I just felt a drop—it's starting to rain."

The heron righted its head and stared into Mica's eyes, and a torrent of images swept into Mica's mind. The young nestling they had used to convince the squire, grown into a majestic female heron. . . . Her flight, across dark forests, high open ridges, from one marsh to another, until she found this coastal marsh. . . . Her presence in this nest raising many broods of birds. . . . This heron, the one staring at him is one of the nestlings of that mother bird. . . . The mother, hunting in the marsh, her foot ensnared in a tangle of branches. . . . The fox, with blue and gray down feathers still clinging to its fur, delivering a meal of freshly killed swamp bird to the kits back in the den.

The heron took three careful steps across the nest, again tilted its head to the left, and a tear dropped on Mica's head. He felt it sink into his scalp, burning ever so slightly, and with it came another flow of images from the heron's mind, like the incoming tide pushing upstream. He sensed the heron's familial gratitude for saving their old rookery.

The heron spoke into his mind, "I give you the gift of flight from tomorrow's dawn until dawn of the following day. May your flight be swift as you retrace my mother's path." Mica knew what they had to do.

When he and Frosten got to the base of the tree, Quartz complained of the slight stinging where the raindrop had fallen. Not understanding the significance, she could already feel a tingle in her fingers. Mica assured her that he had a plan. They supped early and fell into a heavy sleep.

In the distance, we heard a generator engine rumble and settle to a steady drone. The lights in the palapa flickered on just as the episode ended. "Time for dinner," I announced.

"No! We want to find out if they make it back to Cheshire to save Tourmaline," Tara and Eli implored.

"We'll have another episode tonight. I promise." Out into the tropical breeze we trundled, with me in the front to run interference with the land crabs. As I went to bed that night I pondered the mysteries of storytelling. When I'd resumed the story, I hadn't really known the details of what would happen. I knew Quartz and Mica needed to make it back to Cheshire, but I had no idea how they were going to accomplish the task. I was as surprised as they were when Mica suggested asking the heron. Over the past five years, there had been no herons in the story. The backstory about saving the herons had been created as part of Mica's suggestion; it hadn't been part of the previous story line.

Nor had we seen any herons since we'd been in Mexico. They were marsh denizens, and part of the point was to embed New England natural history and ecology (where heron rookeries occur, the functions of wetlands, predator-prey relationships) in the texture of the story. Good storytelling is like jazz improvisation. You know the melody and the direction of the tune, but what happens at any moment comes from somewhere else, from the keyboard or deep down inside or out of the blue, if you open yourself to the muse. Something about the heron motif felt right. But were blue herons part of the local Yucatan fauna?

The next day dawned bright and beautiful. A day of possibility, a day of adventure. On this trip I had discovered and become fascinated by swimming in cenotes, places where underground rivers, flowing through the cavernous Swiss-cheesey limestone of the Yucatan Peninsula, come to the surface. Or where the limestone gets undercut and caves into the flowing water underneath. Some cenotes are well known and touristy, with campesinos charging admission. Others are tucked back in the jungle, accessible only to those willing to ask around and commit to following sketchy paths back into the dense underbrush.

A big group of us had gone to a cenote called the Temple of Doom the day before. Here you had to jump from the limestone edge down into a dark pool fifteen feet below and then climb out via a rickety ladder. The pool you dropped into was much bigger than the limestone opening, which was only about thirty feet across. The inky waters disappeared into the darkness and there were rumors of gators lurking in the shadows. You had to time your jump from the edge just right so you wouldn't collide with the big bats that, disturbed from their sleep, flew off below you seeking a quieter perch. It was creepy and mythic.

Today, Tara and I were heading out on our own. Our funky hotel sat at the northern edge of Sian Ka'an, a newly designated World Biosphere Reserve that stretched for almost a hundred miles southward. The reserve started just a mile or so down the road and encompassed endless stretches of jungle, swamp, empty beaches, and a cenote I'd heard about. Our challenge was to dip our toes into the fringes of this wilderness.

We loaded backpacks, lunch, masks, and fins into our luminescent yellow rented VW Bug and negotiated the potholed road past a few restaurants, ranchitos, and campsites, then slipped into dry, coastal jungle. The trail to the cenote appeared soon, marked by a slim pullout. It wasn't a pretty cenote, and there was no easy access to the water because trees and undergrowth crowded right up to the edge. The open water twisted narrowly around little limestone islands back into overhung channels. I have to confess, it made me a bit queasy. What kinds of poisonous snakes, moray eels, and stinging insects might inhabit this out-of-the-way place? The day before, driving to the hotel, we'd been stopped dead in our tracks by a muscular fifteen-foot boa constrictor crossing the road. I'd never seen a snake that big, even in a herpetorium. I knew I was too big for an alligator, but I wondered if Tara was still within the bite-size range for some hungry reptile hiding under the drooping branches of a gumbo-limbo tree.

I took an exploratory snorkel, saw zillions of fish and nothing predatory, and encouraged Tara into the water. It was spooky, but exhilarating. We swam through shrouds of miniature silvery fish, got little shivers over the shallow ledges where it felt as though something was going to reach up and grab us, and found the underground spring that was the source for this cenote. Hovering above the sandy depression with a cavernous black hole leading down into Hades, we could feel the upward pressure of the spring flow buoy us up, like the lift going over the crest of a roller coaster.

We started to drift back toward our sandals and backpacks when, out of the corner of my eye, in a darkened recess near the bottom, I saw something move that looked much too big to be a fish. It was considerably bigger than me, and it seemed to me to be moving in a surreptitious, ready-to-strike kind of way. I inhaled deeply, announced that we had a full agenda for the day, and hustled us out of there as quickly as I could without letting Tara know that I was the least bit scared. Isn't that what dads are for? But I was left with that "something lurking beneath the surface that I don't understand" feeling for the rest of the day.

We got back in the car and continued south. We were looking for some easy access to the empty shoreline, but a jungly little dune ridge kept the beach frustratingly out of sight. With the engine turned off, we could hear waves in the distance, but there was a seemingly impenetrable thicket between us and paradise. We drove for miles along the monotonous, rutted road. No other cars, and no hints of an opening across the ridge to the beach. Finally I turned around and retreated north, stopping when I found a spot where there was enough room to get the car off the road. It wasn't very far to the beach, and I had faith in my bushwhacking skills. If I marked a path through the thicket, I knew we could find our way back.

We crashed through the saw palmetto, avoided prickly pears and ocotillo, de-snagged ourselves from thorny shrubs. In Boy Scout fashion, I discreetly broke branches, constructed trail arrows, and scratched blazes in bark with a sharp stone. Finally we crested the ridge, thrilled to see that there was only another fifty feet or so to the beach. Where we broke out of the mosquito-infested thicket and into the bright openness of the beach, we created a stick tower to mark the trail entrance.

In both directions, for what seemed like miles, stretched flawless white coral sands and gentle waves. Not a bleached Pepsi can or crushed plastic cup in sight. Serene emptiness. Except, what was that? Maybe three hundred feet down the shore, was that somebody standing in shallow water? We shaded our eyes and strained to pull the image into clarity. A piece of driftwood, a young boy fishing? It was motionless, almost statuesque. We strolled in its direction, letting the waves wash our ankles, letting our eyes search for shells.

When I looked again, the silhouette snapped into recognition. "A blue heron!" I whispered to Tara. We looked at each other in amazement. "The blue heron from the story?" she gasped. I didn't know how to answer.

We sat for a while and watched it. Motionless for long periods of time, then darting its bill into the shallows, pulling out what looked like one of those little silvery fish we had swum amongst in the cenote. We went for a swim and then lay in the sun, and the bird continued to fish, seemingly unaware of our presence. When we walked closer it finally spooked, looped out over the water, circled over us, and drifted down the beach, around a point and out of view.

For the rest of the time we were in Mexico, at least a week, I never saw another blue heron. And though blue herons are commonplace in my neighborhood and in the marshes of New England, I've rarely seen them fishing on the beach edge of the ocean.

Of all those miles of beach we drove along that afternoon, how was it that I chose that nondescript place to pull over and bushwhack out to the beach? Why, when Mica had to devise a solution to the story problem, had he chosen to befriend the heron? Why not an osprey or a broad-winged hawk? If an osprey had appeared in the story, would Tara and I have popped out on the beach to see an osprey swooping into the shallow water to clasp a silvery dorado in its claws before it soared away to a treetop driftwood nest?

Jung called it synchronicity. I've always thought of it as a kind of actualized magic. When I tell stories, I try to enfold recent, everyday events into them. And sometimes elements that pop into a story without planning also have a way of popping into actual events; it happened a number

of times during the Quartz and Mica story cycle. I've come to think of it
as courting magic. If I can attend to the shadows that lurk at the edge of
my consciousness, if I can tell a story and allow natural images to drop
in like unannounced visitors, then the story hums, and everyday events
resonate with it.

THE SYNCHRONICITY DOESN'T STOP THERE. Many years after the experience in Mexico, I'm writing this account one September on Swan's Island,
off the coast of Maine, where I'm renting a friend's house for a weeklong
solo writing retreat. Serene emptiness. Writing and biking. Long days
when I say not a word to another person. Then one day Mike, the guy
my friends hire for maintenance work, shows up to cut the grass. A few
mornings earlier I had unlocked the crawl space to pull out a kayak. I
laid the padlock on the ground and went kayaking, but when I looked
for the padlock later that afternoon, I couldn't find it anywhere. I spent a
half hour searching through the grass and was completely puzzled. How
could the padlock have disappeared?

I've never met Mike before, but I explain the situation and ask him to
keep an eye out for the lock while he's mowing. I return inside to write
about Quartz and Mica and herons and strange coincidences as Mike
trims the lawn. When I hear the engine sputter off, I go out to check with
him. He doesn't seem to be in much of a rush, and, in his deep down east
drawl, he launches into speculation.

"Couldn't find that padlock. Prob'ly the crows got it. They'll pick up
anythin' shiny. People go in the water at the beach and you'll see them
crows pick up their sunglasses while they's out there in the water. I've
seen 'em peckin', peckin', peckin' in the grass and I'll go over and, yup,
there's a dime they's been tryin' to pick up.

"Why, one day when I first come to the island, I was clammin' with
my brother. Workin' out in those flats over by the Carryin' Place. He took
off his class ring from high school and set it on top of his gear so's not to
get it all scratched up. Come back a coupla hours later and 'twas nowhere
to be found. We searched all 'round for it, but then the tide come in.

"Six years later, one of the guys that worked on the Bass Harbor ferry saw something shiny lying on the deck. Stooped down to pick it up. 'Twas a class ring, with my brother's initials on the inside. He was sure happy to get it back. Mighta been those crows.

"You look around here, find a nest, you might find that lock. Course I never seen a crow's nest. Never seen a baby crow for that matter."

How is this happening? I wonder as I listen to his story. Here I am writing about stories and birds and strange coincidences, and he spontaneously launches into a story about birds and strange coincidences. Is this a case of meta-synchronicity? Did my writing encourage Mike to choose this afternoon to come cut the grass? Does he tell that class ring story to everyone? Could a crow really pick up something as heavy as a padlock?

Perhaps I could weave this new bird thread into the nest of the story? To illustrate the principle of working everyday occurrences into stories, I'll slip this bit of crow lore that I just learned from Mike into the next chapter of Quartz and Mica. Let's pick up the story where we left off in Mexico.

Empowered by the heron's gift, Quartz and Mica make the long flight from the coast back to Cheshire. They are hiding out disguised in a village near the castle, trying to hatch a rescue plan for Tourmaline.

Looking out the window at the few free birds left in the forest, Quartz suddenly saw a way they could save Tourmaline from the dragon and his shape-shifting chandelier! Mica's eyes brightened when she whispered her plan, and they immediately set out to recruit a confederate.

The dragon conducted his transformations at sunset, because the chandelier was powered by the green flash of light emitted just as the last bit of sun sinks below the horizon. A complex set of mirrors, perched high on the castle turret, captured the green flash and channeled it down to a central, 99-faceted emerald that served as the igniter for all the emeralds arrayed in the chandelier. As the green flash faded, the chandelier growled to life and an eerie reptilian light shone down on the victim. Five seconds in its glow induced the victim into a powerful hypnotic trance so that the dragon could implant any idea into his brain, and even shift the victim's shape as well as his allegiance. Wily raccoons became placid goldfish; thoughtless rabbits became dragon-loyal wolves. The dragon relished this opportunity to transmute cunning Tourmaline into a simpleton herdsman whom he could use to clean out the horse stalls.

When the belly of the sun touched the horizon, the wolf guards brought Tourmaline to the chamber. Tourmaline struggled, biting and scratching with all his might, but five wolves easily overpowered him. They pinned his arms and legs and positioned his head at the target point of the shaft of reptilian light.

Unbeknownst to the dragon, though, something was happening up above. High on the castle turret a murder of loyal crows protected the mirrors from bird excrement. But on this afternoon one new crow had slipped into their ranks, a crow who did not owe allegiance to the dragon. This crow was a collector of shiny objects—coins, buckles, gold rings, anything that sparkled in the light of the sun. Quartz and Mica had alerted him to the existence of the penultimate shiny object, second only to the sun: the 99-faceted emerald at the core of the chandelier. And when the other crows were briefly blinded by the setting sun, the sparkle crow dropped unseen, down past the mirrors, to the center of the chandelier. Using his beak to pry the gem from its gold setting, the crow snatched it away just as the green flash was plummeting downward.

The dragon watched expectantly to see Tourmaline's angry glare transmute to puppy-dog goofiness. But when the green glow failed to emanate from the chandelier, the dragon jerked his head up and roared, "Who has been tampering with my chandelier?!" His fiery breath exploded upward into the turret, rocketing the crows skyward, their tail feathers singed. "Not us, not us, not us!" they all cawed simultaneously. The crow thief was long gone, eager to stash his treasure in his secret nest.

This episode wasn't in the original telling of the story. I can't really remember how Tourmaline was saved. But this revision illustrates how I typically incorporated odd bits and pieces of our lives into my stories.

When Eli had a dream about a "chicken vampire," the chicken vampire became a comic heroine in the story. When I went sea kayaking in Maine and collected a set of polished, pure white quartz stones, they became divination stones. I kept them in a suede bag and taught Tara to cast spells—of Invisibility, Truth, Strength, Flight—by placing the stones in different configurations. Then, at different points in the story, she'd choose which spell to cast and the story would go in that direction. (The spell idea originated from a computer game she and Eli were intrigued with at the time.)

In such ways the Quartz and Mica story became a crazy quilt of our lives, unique to our experience and places special to us. My hope was that this evolving story would create deep totemic relationships between my children and the natural features and creatures of New England. I was happy to see that it stayed with them even after the telling ended.

When Tara took an advanced art class in high school and needed to choose an animal for a final project, she pored over my guidebooks and eventually chose a blue heron as her subject. She said at the time, "The ongoing epic of Princess Quartz and the corresponding outdoor adventures have taught me to truly adore the natural world and see the characters and personalities of rocks and plants and landscapes."

The Quartz and Mica stories also helped Tara and Eli become storytellers themselves, starting in middle childhood. Tara's casting of spells was one way she started to shape the stories. Or, at certain junctures in the story, I'd give them a choice. Should Mica confront the dragon by himself or wait until the other princes return? At a crossroads, should they head north to the mountains, or south to the marshes? In such ways I was gently handing off the storyteller responsibility to them.

In their own ways, they're both storytellers and adventurers now. Tara writes and directs plays. As a drama teacher at a Maine island school, she works with high school students, helping them tell their own stories and write their own plays. In the summer after his sophomore year of college, Eli directed an adventure program for middle school children at a YMCA camp. His challenge was to explore the nooks and crannies of the Monadnock region—new swimming holes, blueberried summits, the twisty paths at the bear dens. And along the way he entertained them with stories.

I'm hoping that they'll tell the Quartz and Mica stories to my grandchildren—and invite them to add their own characters and plot twists.

Moving in My Heart
A Divorce Mediated by Nature

A week before the earthquake that shook our family, Tara graduated from eighth grade. Her painting was exhibited at the graduation ceremony, a copy of a Renoir that glowed with an arresting inner light. During the proceedings, she spoke with conviction and distinction, her voice clear and articulate. Wendy and I took her out for dinner afterward to tell her how much we respected the young woman she had become. When the salads arrived, I made an emotional speech, the gist of which was that I believed she had embarked as an independent young woman on a path with heart. The moment felt like a completion to me—the end of one phase of fatherhood and moving into the next.

Little did I know. A week later Wendy informed me that we were getting divorced. Not "I think we should consider divorce" or "I'd like to talk about getting divorced." Rather, it was, "We're getting divorced. My mind is made up. I've met with my lawyer and I've chosen a mediator I think we should see. I've arranged to have the house appraised and I've started looking for other places to live." No ifs, ands, or buts.

I was blindsided. ("My lawyer"? I didn't even know Wendy had a lawyer.) Perhaps it was a testament to my insensitivity that I had no idea it was coming. Sure, we had problems in our relationship, but so did every other couple we knew well. I had often said that our marriage and family life were 90 percent great and 10 percent a drag—and, in the big picture, that was pretty good.

I quickly proposed that we go back to a marriage therapist we had seen a few years ago to work on things. I acknowledged all the ways in which I hadn't been the best partner and specified the issues I would try to work on. I apologized for not being attuned to her obvious inner turmoil. But the die had been cast. The thrill and the will to make it work were gone.

The first couple of weeks were ugly, as I oscillated between outrage and guilt, between self-pity and trepidation over telling the kids. I'd hold it together for a few hours and then dissolve in my office, barely able to muffle my sobs. For the first time in my life, I felt my heart breaking, because many of the hopes and dreams that had been the underpinnings of my adult life were shattering before my eyes.

One of my fatherhood promises had always been, "I want my children to leave for college from the same house that they were born in." Both Tara and Eli were born at home, and we were well on the way to realizing that dream. I was committed to being in one place and giving our children deep roots. I'd even chosen the place where I wanted my ashes distributed—a little hemlock grove on the edge of Eliza Adams Gorge, a fifteen-minute walk from our house. And though it sounds corny, when we were driving through Franconia Notch a few years ago and caught a glimpse of the Old Man of the Mountain, Eli said, "It makes me proud to be from New Hampshire," and I choked up. This was the sense of place that I'd been trying to instill in him and Tara. Divorce threatened to pull it up by the roots and let it wither in the sun.

After we told the children what was happening, one of Tara's first exclamations was, "We'll never go for walks to the gorge together again." These walks to the gorge were one of the staples of family life. The forty-minute walk—across the meadow, down the steep hill, up through the hemlocks (future home of my ashes), to the dam at Howe Reservoir, back along a bit of the Monadnock-Sunapee Trail, then left on the road a quarter mile up to the house—was always the same and yet always different. The reservoir was our private family skinny-dipping spot. When the water was high and coming over the dam, you could creep in behind the waterfall, just like in fairy tales.

The gorge provided endless new adventures. We climbed the rock faces, walked across the narrow top of the dam, played Pooh Sticks—throwing sticks into the accelerating current and watching them zoom down the sluiceway into the rapids below. One winter we found a deer carcass below the dam and a dead fisher by the base of the storm-felled beech tree. Whether it was just the four of us together or with big crowds of friends for birthday parties, the gorge had become the emblem of family-place togetherness.

My identity as a father and a family member was all bound up with our home, our yard, and the nearby wilderness of Eliza Adams Gorge. As the children grew older, our explorations spiraled outward, up into the mountains and to the islands along the rocky and sandy coasts. We traveled far afield, but we always came home to the all-together walk to the gorge, back to the secure assuredness of family. It all seemed lost now.

Eventually I got past this darkest view, realizing that even if I couldn't save the marriage, Wendy and I together could try to preserve our children's sense of being loved by both of their parents. And we could save their sense of place, their connectedness to the landscape of the Monadnock region and New England. Wendy and I may have had our differences, but we had been united in our desire to cultivate our children's connection to nature. I had taken the lead in creating adventures; she had been responsible for constructing seasonal rituals.

Wendy found a place to live in Harrisville so the children's friendships and routines would remain intact. Still, the process was going to be emotionally tumultuous, especially for Tara and Eli. Could my fierce commitment to place be one of their lifelines, the thing-to-hold-onto as the ground shook?

By the time Wendy initiated the tectonic shift, most of our plans for that summer were already locked in place. The whole family was to spend a week on the Appalachian Mountain Club's Three Mile Island in Lake Winnepesaukee. Then Tara and I would take a four-day sojourn on Naushon, one of the Elizabeth Islands at the sea end of Buzzards Bay. Later, Eli and I would rent a house with another dad and son on Frenchboro, a tiny offshore community at the outer edges of Blue Hill Bay in Maine. Three affordable island getaways, and yet I was tempted to cancel all of them. Family vacations were the mainstay of our family life. Could we really do it without Wendy?

We'd been to Three Mile Island the year before, but Wendy had joined us only for a couple of days. Whereas the kids and I had a ball, she complained about feeling claustrophobic. She felt too confined, and there was no place for her to do her daily runs. I realized that the pattern had changed in the past few years. In the early years, we had all gone on adventures together. More recently, I would go off on adventures with the kids and Wendy would go off by herself or retreat into a book. The signs were there, and I had been ignoring them.

I reminded myself that our destinations this summer were three remarkably beautiful places, two with memories, one completely new. Perhaps I could dissolve some of the pain of divorce by saturating myself and my children in natural wonder. Could a closeness to beauty be an antidote for loss?

Three Mile Island: Forgetting

It's the last week of July 2001, and I am hoping that the week on Three Mile Island (with Wendy now out of the equation) will grant the gift of forgetting. Wendy's moving-out date is set for August 12, so she's still at home. As the date approaches, the dread increases. I keep hoping that the bad dream will end, that she'll decide to give it one more try. I plead with her to imagine the pain this is causing for the children and me. I try to be especially nice to show her how it can be different. But as she starts to pack up and clean out closets, the illusion of détente diminishes. It's a relief to get away from home.

I pack up Tara and Eli and head for Lake Winnepesaukee early on Saturday morning. At the boat landing, we meet our old family friends Chris and Susan and their two sons, with whom we had planned this vacation. They provide a comforting sense of extended family, and it's good for Eli to have a couple of friends along. As soon as the launch departs for the island, I know we've made the right decision. It's a sparkly day; Mount Chocorua beckons on the horizon. My whole body exhales deeply. The sunlight off the lake massages some of the tension from my shoulders, and the persistent tightness in my throat softens. I trickle out of my head and back into my body. The first taste of wind washes the kids' faces.

On the island we are swept up in a swoop of activities: long-distance swimming, kayaking, canoeing, dock games, tennis. There's a clump of ten- to twelve-year-old kids, and Eli, as one of the oldest and coolest, becomes the ringleader. Tara finds a group of teens to gallivant around with late at night. Much to my surprise, there are other divorcées with their families. I'm not alone! And though my mother was a serious alcoholic and I have never been a drinker, I find that getting mildly sloshed during the impromptu happy hour at a different cabin each evening is just the ticket for easing the pain.

Yet the dominant note is serenity. Each two-person sleeping cabin (with space for not much more than two beds, a set of drawers, and a chair) is a world unto itself. There's a porch, a tiny private dock, a soft forest of pines and hemlocks, and only kerosene lighting. It's really hot, so Eli and I take a late-night swim right before bed each night, picking our way carefully across the pine-needled granite down to our dock and slipping into the ink-dark water. We swim in stars and then flop onto the weathered boards to dry, the lantern-lit cabin hovering invitingly above us. "I love this place," Eli whispers, mostly to himself. Our sorrows drip off our bodies, through the gaps between the dock boards, and get lost in the lake.

My more conscious strategy is Daddy's Sailing Camp. There's no formal daily schedule, but I have committed myself to teaching Tara and Eli to sail. I figure that learning to sail will both preoccupy us and provide a path into the new terrain ahead. In the tumult of change, I sense that we need new skills to get us unstuck and provide forward momentum.

The Sunfishes sit rigged and ready to go at the boat slip near the main dock. It's easy to be out on the water in less than five minutes. I do a separate tutorial with each of the kids. On Eli's first day the winds are light. I take the rudder, and he takes the sail. It's pleasant and a little boring, but he gets the feel and it's doable. The next day we wait till the afternoon thermals pick up. We quickly get the boat up on edge and I teach him how to hike out. His face is alive with exhilaration. I have him take the sail, though in strong gusts he quickly hands it back to me. But the edginess appeals to him; the hook has been set.

The third day, after a Canadian front has moved through, there's a good stiff northwesterly breeze. Today I have him take the tiller and, after a bit, hand him the sail. He keeps wanting to push it back into my hands, but I won't take it. We almost dump a couple of times, and yet we let the sail out, clarify the options in dicey situations, and keep going. He doesn't want to come about in really stiff gusts, but I assure him he can do it. After he pulls it off smoothly, with both of us ducking and shifting our weight in harmony, he gets a big smile on his face. I realize we're replaying the dynamics of divorce, initially awkward and clumsy in that new landscape, buffeted by squalls of emotion, and slowly figuring out how to adapt to a new place.

We go back and forth on the same tack a number of times, and gradually a settled assuredness enters into his demeanor. As we're heading back in, though, a bolt slips loose from the rudder and disappears into the depths, making the boat unsteerable, and we have to improvise—just as we're doing in our emotional lives every day. I swim the boat in for the last couple hundred yards while he manages the sail, and we wind up feeling proud of how we dealt with this little emergency.

Over these five or six days of sailing camp, a lot of the discussion is about wind direction, hiking out, the physics of how the sail converts the wind into forward momentum, how to right the boat if it flips. I conduct a similar set of lessons with Tara, and though it's not as intuitive for her as it is for Eli, she too starts to get it. I'm hoping that the metaphors are working on them in a subtle, subconscious way, so I refrain from being overt about it. Instead, we just eat and drink sailing, our personal lotus blossoms, and we forget about Penelope, who is not waiting longingly for us to return home.

This is only part of the picture, of course. I cry a little every day. I wince as I walk past moms and dads splashing playfully with their little ones. When I walk behind Chris and Susan and he takes her hand on the way to dinner, I long for closeness. When I talk about my sadness or anger, Tara tells me to suck it up, to stop being morose. We lash out at each other and then make up. But, in a small way, the wind in our boat sails actually puts wind in our inner sails, and we get pulled out of the doldrums of depression. Tara, Eli, and I bond as a threesome and find a unique bit of personal independence in our sailing skills. We move forward.

Naushon: Remembering

We go home for a week, and then Tara and I head off to Naushon on a mission of remembering. I'd been here a few times before, once on an idyllic getaway with Wendy during our courtship. I sense that the emotional task here is going to be different.

At the Steamship Authority dock in Woods Hole, we avoid the mobs of tourists pouring onto the mega-ferries heading to Martha's Vineyard and Nantucket. Instead, we find our way to Track 9½ and slip onto the secret little boat heading for Naushon. Though it's only a thirty-minute ride, we arrived at a place almost as otherworldly as Hogwarts. Tara described it this way: "You know how you go into a museum and there's a diorama of a long-ago coastal village? Everything is just so, the houses are cute, there are tiny sheep in the meadows, horse-drawn carriages on the lanes, and you wish you could shrink down and walk into that world to live for a few days. That's what being on Naushon is like."

Naushon is a family-and-friends-only place, and we're not family, but we've lucked out and managed to get invited by friends to stay at Tarpaulin Cove. It's a four-mile hike down the island, three and a half miles beyond all the other houses, so we're heading into one of New England's most pristine time warps. Weaving through ancient beech and holly forests, past abandoned sheep enclosures, down through druidic copses of ancient oaks, along salt-marsh-edged beaches, we arrive at a nineteenth-century farmhouse and barns that have barely changed in the past century. There's a little solar electricity and a hand pump for water. The old post office is still in the parlor; the furniture is tattered. Except for having to pick 127 ticks off of my socks and sneakers upon arrival, it's darn close to beauty.

Tara and I spend the next three days wandering the labyrinth of trails on the west end of the island in complete solitude. One seamless day we're out for six hours and never see another person. We leave the farm and follow the Fox Holes Path down through tucked-away meadows to Crescent Beach, a half-mile-long, resort-worthy strand. Though Tara and I have always been great companions, we have to find a way of being together in this post-mommy-and-daddy world. We collect beach glass, make tiny balanced stone sculptures, cup comb jellies in our hands when we swim in the Bahamas-clear water. Blissful oblivion.

But here the task isn't about forgetting, it's about remembering. It's about starting to make peace with the past. As we picnic, Tara asks about my favorite foods, and right away I think of curried chicken barley soup. And since we're in no rush, I describe the memory it brings forth.

When Tara was just a year old, I took a leave of absence from my job, and Wendy, Tara, and I lived in Great Britain for half the year. Wendy describes it as one of the best times of our marriage. We began in Scotland, renting a house on Harris, way offshore in the outer Hebrides. With Tara in the backpack, we went for long, drizzly, wool-sweater-and-raincoat walks through sheepy, heathy highlands. We lurked around ceremonial stones, shopped for tweeds, and drank a lot of tea. Since Tara would bounce and shriek in the backpack whenever we encountered flocks of woollies in the heather, we made up a song about her that included this refrain:

She will shriek and she will wail
And she'll make the north wind fail
She's the wee siren of the Hi-igh-lands.

The song seemed to embody all our love for Tara and our hopes and dreams as a new family. At the end of those gray, windswept walks, we'd return to our croft, and Wendy's curried chicken barley soup took the chill out of our bones.

I hide my tears from Tara with my bent arm across my face, and am overwhelmed with questions I hadn't anticipated. What do I do with all the memories? Does the dissolution of the marriage relegate all these wonderful memories to the ash heap? How do I integrate the current pain with all the recollected happiness? We talk about why I am crying, and Tara, in her young wisdom, says something like, "It was good then, and it's not good now. They both exist, and we have to figure out a way to not have the pain take away the good memories." Thank you, Siddhartha, I say to her in gentle jest. On the walk back, we make a plan to work on the memories.

Back at the farmhouse, she heads off to collect blueberries and I go after blackberries—about a quart altogether. As our hostess Daphne and her mother prepare pasta and garlicky, fresh mussels, Tara and I work on the dessert. One of Wendy's vacation specialties was a scrumptious blackberry-blueberry tart with a few flourishes. Before our marriage I had been a reasonable cook, but since Wendy was much better at it, I gradually let her take over most of the dinner cooking. I was a master at breakfasts and lunches, but whenever she wanted us to cook dinner together, I avoided it. It was one of my failings in the marriage to not join her in the kitchen. I decide to begin my rehabilitation.

I choose to make a *pâte sucrée* crust, following the directions in *The Joy of Cooking*. Tara works on the filling, cooking the berries only slightly with sugar. Wendy's special twist was a thin layer of dark chocolate and coconut underneath the filling. With cocoa powder and butter, I create a reasonable facsimile. Since I haven't worked with tart crust in years and we talk endlessly about each step, it takes hours.

The tart is a raving success, even though it leaks a bit of chocolate-berry blood when we slice it. Toasted coconut decorates the top. The gently browned tart crust slips gracefully away from the pan. With a dash of yogurt, it tastes divine. For Tara and me, it is an homage to Mommy. Making her tart is a way of making her present for us, affirming the memory, expressing our love for her. For me, it's a conscious counterpoint to the bitterness I feel. Bittersweet. I am trying to balance my anger toward her with an appreciation of how she sweetly shaped all of our lives. It's also a coming out, choosing to reclaim the mommy side of myself, deciding to mend my ways.

On our last day, we rise at 5:00 A.M. in order to catch the 8:30 boat. We swim in the before-dawn stillness, eat granola, and hit the trail. Deer dart off into the woods in front of us. We walk in silent beauty. As we wait for the boat, Tara says, "I thought it was going to be a lot harder, but I'm not that sad. I don't feel heartbroken." And even though my heart does still feel broken, we've started to bake the memories into new possibilities.

Frenchboro: New Sensations

Wendy moves out of the house a couple of days later, with help from Tara. The house both our children were born in, the house we'd done seven different renovations on, the house I thought we'd live in till death do us part. I am still acclimating to the quick oscillation between joy and despair. In fact, when someone asks me later what I've learned through this whole process, I find myself saying that I've learned that emotional states aren't exclusionary. Joy and melancholy can exist simultaneously, with neither of them depleting or amending the other. Just as I have come to accept that there will always be an ache or a pain somewhere in my body when I wake up in the morning, I have accepted that my longing for a complete family will always be naggingly present at the periphery of my emotional consciousness.

The ferry from Bass Harbor on Mount Desert Island goes to Frenchboro only three days of the week. Eli and I arrive in a long, narrow harbor with a 1950s down east lobstering community strewn along the shores. No store, a public school attended by about eight kids, lots of wild shoreline to roam. Unlike the previous islands, Frenchboro is a completely new place, and this adventure is just for us. Emotionally, too, it feels like new terrain—a little scary but exciting. Like not knowing what my new life, as a part-time dad without Wendy, is going to be like. For the first few days, thankfully, Eli and I are not going it alone: Toby, my best friend, who's also in the throes of divorce, and his son Brooks, arrive simultaneously. For a week we've got a funky rental house with a view, loads of food, a flotilla of kayaks, a boathouse and huge dock filled with lobster traps, piles of lumber, tarps, and spare tires. It's a veritable playground for guys on the loose.

One evening we stroll out through the ledgy spruce woods to Little Beach and wait for it to get completely dark. Then we walk back the quarter mile without using our flashlights at all. In the deep woods it's as pitch-black as the inside of a closet. We inch along, finding the path with our feet, snuggling up close to each other for reassurance. We trip over protruding branches, stumble down forgotten ledges, wander off into squishy mini-bogs. Eli slips ahead unnoticed, hides, and then scares the bejesus out of Toby by grabbing him from behind a fallen tree. When we finally reach the gravel road, there's a bit of light overhead and we walk easily, amazed that we actually did it. Scary and exciting.

Midway through the week, Toby and Brooks depart, leaving Eli and me alone. It's a microcosm of divorce—a big happy family and then life is sucked away. Just the two of us. That day, we mope around, feel depressed, get on each other's nerves. We realize we need to get out.

We set out the next day to an unexplored part of the island, even though the lowering sky suggests rain. On the cobble beach at Eastern Cove, we play the rock-bounce game, one we invented as a family on another Maine island. You toss a nicely rounded stone into a cluster of boulders and watch it boundingly ricochet up, around, and sideways across the shore. We score each rock as though we're scoring Olympic divers, taking into account duration, oddness of bounce, and interesting clatter. We take the average of our scores and the thrower with the highest accumulated score wins. (After all, we're guys.)

We invent a new rock game. We stack a tower of flat stones twenty feet below us on the beach, then take turns trying to knock the tower down. There's something special about this rock game time. Eli appreciates it when I slow down enough to get into kid mode; I appreciate his willingness to work with me to refine the rules. Because we're by ourselves, without Tara or Wendy, we're able to settle into this place and into our relationship. The unique qualities of the beach, the cobble boulders, and the steep pitch of the shore bring Eli and me to a new place of colleagueship. As in our night walk, new sensations can emerge from a walk in the darkness of divorce.

We clamber along the shore for a couple of miles until a squall blows in. At Bluff Head, Eli suggests hanging out under some primeval lichen-festooned trees, but then it starts to rain seriously. Striking out in what appears to be the right direction to get back to our car, we bushwhack through gloomy, unendingly similar mossy woods and blowdown. Our faces are streaked with wet needles, the trails are poorly marked, it's a long way from home, and we're having a blast. When we stumble on a little trail intersection we recognize from about four hours ago, we look at each other gleefully. Slogging the half mile back to the car, pleased as punch, I realize that I'm starting to think of Eli less as a son and more as a friend, a potential companion for the long haul. We're finding our way together in this new terrain.

That afternoon we make apple pie together in liberated, new-age-guy fashion. Now the dreariness of the drizzle accentuates the warm glow we feel inside. Eli's class recently made a big batch of pies for a school event, so he's reminding me how to make crust—another father-son reversal, an opening into new aspects of our selves. When I ask, "On a scale of one to ten, with sadness being one and happiness being ten, where would you place yourself?" I'm surprised when he says, seven or eight. I think to myself, we're going to make it through this.

Postscript: A Summer Later

Summer passes into fall and the hard work begins. Wendy lives about three miles away and we share the kids evenly. I hate the feeling of being a part-time father: too hectic, then too isolated. When the kids leave on Sunday, it's like a knife driven into my chest. Wendy wants to fast-track the whole divorce process, so by April it's signed, sealed, and delivered. The kids, all things considered, hold up quite well, even flourish at times. For me, it's baby steps. My resentment toward Wendy and my embarrassment at failing at marriage recede at a glacial pace.

June and July are busy work months, and then Tara and Eli and I return to Three Mile Island. It feels like a homecoming. And it's a relief to recognize how different we feel from one year ago, when we were all still reeling. Tara is her old smiley self and quickly connects with the camp crew because, serendipitously, one of her former boyfriends from school is on the kitchen staff.

One night, just after midnight, she checks in with me and returns to her cabin about seventy-five yards down the shore from mine. There's the reassuring bang of the screen door, but then I hear her dive into the lake, and then there's another dive into the lake. Hmm. Twenty minutes later I shuffle down the trail and yell to her, suggesting that her nighttime visitor should depart reasonably soon. For much of the week she's off with friends, and though I miss hanging out with her, her buoyant independence is invigorating.

On the morning of the third day, I wake up humming the refrain from one of the Sunday night hymn-sing selections. It's an old gospel song:

Every time I feel the spirit
Moving in my heart, I will pray.

I don't quite know what it means, but it's clear it's reverential, and I do feel some kind of spirit moving in my heart. When I'm alone, I belt it out with basso resonance, over and over. I make it my mantra.

Sailing camp resumes. One afternoon the wind is humming, causing whitecaps, short steep waves, and nearly a small-craft warning. Eli wants to take his friend Joschka out. This is way more wind than Eli has ever sailed in, but I decide to let them go, and Joschka's parents agree. I approach the staff person who's in charge of boats and warn her to get ready for a rescue. I'm nervous—I'm sure they're going to tip over, and in this much of a blow it will be hard to get the boat back up—but I'm willing to let him take the risk.

Out into the teeth of the wind they go. They're riding a bucking bronco and yet they don't get thrown. Eli does absolutely everything right, and they come back in wide-eyed and ecstatic. That evening, after our swim, we stretch out naked on our beds in the flickering lamplight and Eli waxes giddy and grandiloquent:

> If I could sail for a whole day in a wind like that, I'd skip Christmas. It's much more fun, and you don't get to whoop at Christmas and you don't get water splashed in your face. And knowing you could flip it, might flip it, but just not flipping it. Sailing is like chess because it's tactical and there's all these things running through your head, but even then your mind feels clear.

I am amazed at his rush of words. He's not usually this talkative. He clearly felt the spirit out there. He's quiet for a while, and then, almost to himself, he says under his breath, "Skiing and sailing are like a release from the real world. No worries, a meditation, being in the moment there and then. No thinking about the war on terrorism, George Bush, divorce, school. It's all *now*."

It's all now. Two Siddharthas, I think to myself. Maybe that's what this has all been about. Maybe it's the nowness of almost flipping, whooping, clatter of rocks on cobble, swimming in before-dawn stillness, chocolate-berry blood, that loosens the shackles of sadness. I'm learning to let go of my marriage because I can hold on tight to the landscapes of home. And

I'm thrilled to see my children finding their own inner stabilities, keels sunk deep in the blue.

Down deep, we're all wedded to the wind, waters, sand, and stars of New England and the widening world. Till death do us part.

PART THREE

adolescence on the rocky ridge

PRELUDE

IN EARLY CHILDHOOD, the child bonds with the family and develops empathy with nature. In middle childhood, she bonds with the earth, moving outward from the family to explore the real physical worlds of forest, stream, beach, and street. In adolescence, the developmental task is to bond with the self, and the natural world can provide the setting and opportunity for challenging rites of passage.

The adolescent self needs to find a voice. In many traditional cultures, children around the age of puberty participate in a socially designed rite of passage that is structured by adults but requires the young person to go out into the wilderness on his own, find his own path. The individual begins the rite as a child, undergoes some transformation in a physical and spiritual challenge, and emerges as an adult, ready to take on new responsibilities. In parenting Tara and Eli, I tried to create varied opportunities for such supported rites of passages.

It's axiomatic that the transformation during puberty from middle childhood to adolescence can be emotionally challenging, fraught with anxiety about leaving the safety of childhood for the ambivalence of adolescence. Tara, for example, was in a charmed place at the end of middle childhood. At dinner a month before her eleventh birthday, she announced enthusiastically and out of the blue, "I love my life!" A few weeks later, when she noticed it had started to rain, she ran outside, turned cartwheels, and pranced in the twilight, then came back in with the dampness glistening on her face.

But then we got a hint of ambivalence setting in. For Tara's eleventh birthday we watched a charming little film called *Toothless,* in which Kirstie Alley plays a dentist who dies and whose assignment in Purgatory is to be the tooth fairy. Children who have some baby teeth left can see her, but when they insist on her existence, the adults presume that they are just being silly or are seriously off their rockers. At the end of the movie, a boy who has formed a close relationship with the tooth fairy loses his last baby tooth, immediately loses the ability to see the tooth fairy, and forgets that he *ever* could see her. It's a provocative symbol of the end of childhood, the loss of connection to the world of imagination.

Though there's a happy ending, Tara was noticeably upset when the movie was over. She couldn't say why, but I realized that the convergence of the movie and her birthday was striking a disturbing chord for her. As we talked about the movie, she started to sob and finally said, "I like my life just the way it is and I don't want it to change and I don't want to leave you and I don't want you to die. I want things to stay exactly the way they are." I cried too, because I shared her ambivalence about her growing up.

The ages of ten and eleven have classically been considered the golden age of childhood. It's when everything comes together, when ideally there's balance, coordination, and a sense of joy at being in the world. Think of Pippi Longstocking or Caddie Woodlawn or Little Red Riding Hood—strong, capable girls at the end of middle childhood, secure in their bodies and their sense of self. Carol Gilligan and other feminist developmental theorists have pointed to the ways in which girls in particular flourish in late childhood. By eleven they tend to be physically and emotionally sturdy, self-assured, and confident, but then at twelve or thirteen, they go underground and lose their forthrightness. That assuredness starts to deteriorate; the storms of puberty and adolescence roil the clarity about themselves that girls have in late childhood.

I didn't want that to happen with Tara. And much of how I've parented has been in anticipation of this issue. I especially didn't want her and Eli to lose their strong connection with nature as they sprouted a new web of social connections. This kind of shift is partly inevitable, since for many children the almost mythic experience of deep union with nature is linked with the relative solitude of earlier childhood. The British educator James Britton tells how his daughter had been a "woods girl," roaming the forest, but realized she was changing. She says,

> Fourteen is an age at which one decides to become civilized, and the ancient, beautiful, secret Pictish things have to be given up in favour of a more sociable, sophisticated world where friends and people and laughing are all important. It is a change from the outdoor world to the indoor. I can remember moments of such wonderfulness at the top of the sycamore and elm trees that I don't want to spoil—the seriousness and the feeling that I am not a modern girl but something which fits in completely with the wind and the crisp smell of the air and the pattern of the leaves against the sun. I wouldn't be able to feel that again. There is only one thing that still works, and that is lighting a fire in the garden, in the evening, preferably twilight. Sunset used to be almost enchanted, when I was nine or ten. Now there is always part of me holding back and laughing at it.
>
> When I was younger, I could afford to be, and was, lonely. Now people, and friends, and people such as teachers, with whom there is an unnatural sort of relationship, are much more interesting and vital. You have to learn to put up with one person's obstinacy, another's silliness, etc., and still like them, and also to decide what sort of image of yourself you are going to project.

This transition into the social world of peers, along with separating from adults, is unavoidable, but parents can sustain a healthy balance by consciously attempting to keep children connected to the natural world.

Adolescents also have a biological thirst for risk and adventure that many wind up acting out in unhealthy ways. Adult-supported rites of passage can provide opportunities to embrace challenge in ways that don't eliminate risk but instead balance the benefits and the risks. Children are heading up onto the rocky ridge whether we like it or not, so if we can accompany them partway, we can prepare them to encounter risk thoughtfully.

My strategy was to forge a relationship with both my children built on shared adventures outdoors. If I could give them that sense of inner strength that comes from wisely choosing personal challenges and meeting them, perhaps they would stay aboveground rather than going underground. I wanted them to stay communicative, accessible, willing to converse about their challenges and issues. If we practiced meeting challenges together, then perhaps I could gently let them go off to take risks on their own at the appropriate time.

One of my chief methods of trying to guide Tara and Eli up and over the rocky ridge was to deeply cultivate a love of downhill skiing with them. Skiing provides not only opportunities to measure and meet risk, to develop balance and confidence in a dangerous situation, but also an invaluable physical metaphor for children to carry with them. I remember Tara's tears of pride and joy the day she skied Tamarack at Stratton Mountain—her first serious black diamond run—and her exhilaration at age twelve as she described skiing Goosebumps at Mount Sunapee, a double black diamond that she had feared until then: "I did it. I overcame my fear! It wasn't even that hard." She was master of her own destiny; I hadn't even been there to encourage her. Ever-harder skiing challenges gave Tara and Eli a deep inner sense of competence while their bodies and social relationships changed, helping them carry the assuredness of late childhood into the self-doubt stages of adolescence. They also served as a touchstone for our shared experiences.

This contrasts with the way in which many boys and girls process these changes in adolescence. As their bodies change and sexual hormones are added to the mix, they begin to define themselves in terms of their attractiveness and relationships to others. Romance becomes a prominent vehicle for self-development. Though this has to happen, there's no value in having it happen sooner rather than later. Instead we should be encouraging adolescents to identify and follow their inner passions—becoming good musicians or artists or mathematicians or skiers or field hockey players. With my children, I tried to hone their outdoors skills as a vehicle for personal identity.

While Tara was in early puberty, I also resisted allowing her to see movies that glorified romance, such as *Titanic*. Clearly many parents avoid violent movies, but I also think it's important to limit the diet of movies that suggest that the sole path of adult development is through a romantic relationship. Of course, this goes hand in hand with the emphasis on appearance, slenderness, and trendy clothes for girls and a similar focus on sports, machismo, and financial success for boys. It's all the more reason to limit children's exposure to excessive television in late childhood and early adolescence.

But the transition is biologically driven and inevitable, and there are good ways for us to meet it. Margaret Mead, in her study of adolescent girls in Samoa in the 1920s, asks, "Are the disturbances which vex our adolescents due to the nature of adolescence itself or to the civilization? Under different conditions does adolescence present a different picture?" Based on her observation of Samoan girls, she felt that there was not a great difference between girls before and after puberty. She concluded that it was American culture that created adolescent angst. My sense has been that the turmoil and anger of adolescence are in small part hormonal and biological, and in large part a cultural artifact. In many ways, as parents and as a society, we create the problems of adolescence; conversely, we can create the different conditions Mead refers to. Perhaps if we did it right in schools, in our families, and in our communities, we could mitigate these problems.

The natural developmental transition into adolescence needs to be acknowledged and supported. Formalizing the end of childhood and the beginning of adulthood through ritual has been an integral part of tradi-

tional cultures. Children need such rites of passage—and, indeed, invent
their own when they're not culturally provided. In urban settings, the
gang provides some of the same meaning as the warrior initiation in traditional cultures. In rural areas, boys set themselves physical challenges
to test their mettle. The high jump off a ledge into the swimming hole sig-
nifies the transition from boy to man. I have even found that some girls
create personally meaningful doll funerals. Realizing that it was time to
put her childhood to rest, one girl described how she took one of her
favorite dolls, cut off its hair, and found a place in the woods to bury it.
This ritual signified the death of her little-girl-playing-with-dolls self.

More formalized rituals for young adolescents are slowly enjoying
a resurgence. Sometimes ancient, cross-cultural rituals based on wilderness experiences have been given new life and form. Kroka Expeditions,
a wilderness adventure organization in New Hampshire, provides many
such opportunities for adolescents, as does the Wilderness Awareness
School and other nature mentoring programs. Another rite of passage
program, called Rediscovery, has emerged among First Nation communities in Canada. Rediscovery staff, with the guidance of Native elders,
blend wilderness and cultural activities to develop and strengthen confidence and self-worth in both Native and non-Native participants. These
and other endeavors, such as the more theatrical Wayfinder Experience,
offer opportunities for adolescents to find themselves through both social
engagement and solo experiences in wilderness settings.

The chapters that follow describe various rites of passage my children
experienced—some with me, some on their own. "Assessing Ice" focuses
on a series of ice-skating adventures Tara and I undertook the winter
when she was thirteen. The subtext is about learning to assess risk in
both natural and social situations when you're on your own.

"Doing Tuckerman's" is the father-son parallel to the preceding chapter. Since this adventure at age twelve, my son has gone on to become a
competitive freestyle skier, mastering some of the gnarliest terrain across
New England and in the West. Skiing Tuckerman's Ravine was the original keyhole for him.

As older teenagers become young adults, parent-child relationships should change. "The Door in the Rock" describes my attempt to move from a parent-child to a collegial relationship with Tara through canyoneering challenges in which both she and I were equally unskilled and on edge.

"Bow Loop and Brimstone" is a parenting swan song. It's an affirmation of the adults my children have become and the nature-oriented aesthetics and commitments they carry with them.

Assessing Ice
Risk and Reward on Skates

A Wallace Stevens poem called "The Snowman" has been snagged in my mind for the last fifteen years, about as long as my family and I have been heading to the Caribbean for a couple of weeks after Christmas each year. As the solstice approaches, I recite the first line, "One must have a mind of winter / To regard the frost and the boughs / Of the pine-trees crusted with snow," and I welcome the sparse truth of leaflessness, the relaxing of preparation. Heading south has increasingly felt like a bioregional betrayal to me, a slap in the face of winter mind, a seasonal sin. Just as the quiet settles like a heavy quilt and the lakes drift off to sleep, I hearken to the beat of the steel drum and toss down piña coladas. "It just isn't natural," whispers the little angel on my shoulder. "Have you forgotten your pledge of allegiance to the snow queen?"

And so I feel a bit embarrassed as we jet off to Tobago, Vieques, or Providenciales to snorkel, surf, and dine on grilled kingfish with mango salsa. Descend jungle trails to coral coves of sugar sand and plunge into rebellious mambo waves that have never learned good manners, never had to sit quietly in one place and be seen and not heard.

The freeze came hard and fast in mid-December 1998. After weeks of relative warmth, the temperature plunked down to below zero for three nights in a row with no wind. The waters bowed obsequiously—yes, Master!—and prostrated themselves. Black ice slithered across the shallower ponds. I ignored the road and glanced through the trees down to Robb Reservoir as I drove to work, and a hunger rose in me when this first pure ice appeared. I left work a bit early on a Friday and used the lingering twilight to check the ice on Child's Bog. Three or four inches of spooky transparency: daunting to the nerves but satin to the skate blades.

That Saturday, Tara and her friend Erin joined me in the first exploration. We were tentative in the beginning. Down on hands and knees to check the depths of the cracks, cautious around stumps and boulders, hesitant as we moved farther away from shore, flinching at the rolling thunder of ice expansion. But as it became apparent that it was unquestionably solid everywhere, we became giddy and playful. We circumnavigated the long cove-y shoreline, weaving in and out of fallen trees that stuck out of the ice. We lay face down and peered into the inky depths and licked the ice, hoping our tongues wouldn't stick. We linked arms and coordinated strides, we raced between outcrops, we tried to make the perfect set of lilting blade marks. Finding the absolute middle of the pond, we lay on our backs and took in the full saucer of spruce-rimmed sky.

In January, when we returned from our Caribbean idyll, the ice was gone, buried under soggy snow, never to reappear again that winter. We paid homage to winter in our downhill skiing adventures, but a piece of me missed the ice, missed the playful explorations with Tara.

As the following December unfolded, cold, still, and snowless, the opportunity for absolution unfolded as well. Encountering ice that millennial December coincided directly with Tara encountering adolescence. Middle childhood had been about experiencing that deep interpenetration of self and wildness. I had tried to help my children develop physical competence as the foundation for a firm sense of self. For us that meant plunging into the water three seasons of the year and embracing winter sports—learning to ski and taking advantage of the short, wild ice season that typically ran from December into early January. The ice-skating experiences we strode into this winter were part of that physical engagement with winter, but a new note, a change of parenting challenge, was emerging as well.

Over the years that Tara moved toward and through puberty, the persistent developmental question for me was this: Does adolescence have to be a time of turmoil and angry separation from parents? I'd be talking with other parents about enjoying cooking dinner with Tara, or about a charming Thanksgiving morning walk we enjoyed. "How old is Tara now?" they'd ask. When I replied that she was thirteen, they'd respond, "Oh, you're just getting to the hard part, the things-fall-apart years. Just you wait!" I nodded in acquiescence, acknowledging the cultural myth, but inwardly I resisted. I am not convinced that things have to fall apart.

During skating that year, the feeling was one of togetherness and collaboration. We were bound together in exploratory spirit, goading each other to go around the next corner, see what was up that little stream. Truth be told, I didn't consciously set out to conduct an ice-skating clinic to prepare her for future challenges. But as the adventures unfolded, adventures she seemed to hunger for, the opportunities for passing on wisdom became apparent.

Skate Away Home

"More confirmation of global warming," we all grumbled as November 1999 stretched on, warm and dry. But then winter snapped its fingers in mid-December, bestowing a quick, hard freeze without a hint of snow. I waited in anticipation, looking for frozen coves, evaluating the shape and size of the patches of open water. Each morning I'd poke a stick through the skim of ice on the frog pond—only a half inch, barely more than an inch. When it warmed up to the thirties and forties, I regretted the setback. But then a few days before the solstice, the temperature suddenly dropped below zero. Some people wait for four inches of ice. I'm comfortable with three if we're staying close to shore, and will consider two when the body of water is small and only waist deep.

I talked Eli into the inaugural skate. By 9:00 P.M., the fullest moon of the century, high in the solstice night sky, was floodlighting the pond. Avoiding the end down by the big rock, where a spring keeps the ice mushy at the beginning of the season, we swooped and scraped, finding our skating legs after almost a year. Cold butts sitting on the ice, we speculated that we might be the only people skating that night, because none of the larger bodies of water were solid enough. It was too cold for more than a short skate, but it whetted my appetite. This winter, for the first time in almost fifteen years, we weren't going south. Perhaps this winter, we could really skate.

DECEMBER 25.   On Christmas day we have a rowdy game of hockey with three families of moms and dads, boys and girls age eight to fourteen, at a friend's house in Peterborough. Lots of bumps and bruises, but mostly the excitement of friendly competitiveness, of parents and children embraced in good-natured tussling. The edginess of fast hockey, of imagining elbows hitting ice, of cold-bitten toes and frosted noses, makes us glow with exhilaration. Pond hockey feels like part of the birthright of a northern New Englander (as in, north of the Mason-Dixon line that is the Massachusetts border). You have to know and trust ice, and abandon yourself to intuitive skating, to succeed at hockey. It's rough, ragged, and exhausting—the crucible of true grit. I love seeing Tara mix it up and steal the puck from one of the dads and whip around to take a shot on goal.

DECEMBER 30.   After a couple of shorter outings, the next-to-last day of the millennium dawns still and warm. "Highs in the upper twenties" is music to our ears. Twenty-nine degrees is the grail temperature for exploratory skaters: cold enough to keep the ice intact, warm enough to feel cozy once the blood gets pumping. Tara willingly takes up my invitation to foray back up the stream that feeds into Harrisville Pond, a long, slightly risky skate this early in the winter. The moving water of the marshy stream, especially over the frequent beaver dams, will make for thin ice and constant vigilance.

We park at the public beach on the pond near the center of Harrisville—an old haunt. Tara has grown up here, learning to swim, collecting small garnets at the water's edge, picking blueberries, experimenting with distance swimming. We lace up at the picnic table, clomp across the sand, and pick our way over the refrozen, wave-driven slush for the first couple hundred yards. But then it's as if the courtiers have rolled out the velvet carpet for the queen; the black ice is immaculate. Beyond the point where she swam out to last summer, her horizon of personal exploration, the familiar starts to fade.

As we approach the mouth of the stream, I explain the challenges ahead. We discuss the strategies of assessing ice, of regularly checking cracks to determine depth, of looking for changes in the surface texture that suggest water movement underneath. We discuss the wisdom of carrying a long branch to catch on the ice in case of a breakthrough and to push off the bottom to get back onto the ice. We plan for what to do if you're trying to rescue someone who has broken through—remain calm, spread out your weight as much as possible, don't get too close to the edge of the broken ice so you don't go in as well. In part, I am training her in close observation of the subtleties of the landscape. It is a seminar in risk assessment; it's about knowing that it's fun to push the limits and sneak back into inaccessible places, and about knowing the limits to pushing, knowing when to say no, this isn't safe anymore. This time I'm not just doing the risk-benefit analysis myself, but also inviting her into the process.

Tara remembers it this way:

As an end to this century and a beginning of the next, Daddy and I have decided to go on as many skating expeditions as we can before the ice turns bad. Today was a good one to start them off. We went to Harrisville Pond, a place I thought I knew, but I found it unseemingly mysterious. We laced up our skates and glided back to where a small stream flows in. Avoiding thin ice and small sections of open water, we made our way back through brush and reeds and sometimes over land. It was quite scary, though the day was bright and clear, looking down and seeing through the ice to where the rushes on the bottom swayed in the current. By moving steadily, lying spread-eagle when we crossed, constantly checking the depth of the ice, and skating extremely slowly and cautiously, we made it successfully back to where the stream got too thin to keep going. Here we lay down on the ice, faces toward the sun, and recollected good times of the past century that we had shared together. We then skated back with a sense of freedom, not having to pay attention to every crossing point in the stream. A happy way to end a happy year.

We dawdle on the way back. The stillness of the afternoon reminds me of slack tide, those few moments after the tide has stopped coming in and hasn't yet started going out. The breeze drops, ceaselessness ceases, time naps. Coming upon a rope swing, we use it to make ourselves into drawing compasses and inscribe geometrical circles in the ice. We skate by Jack's place, and Tara points out the fallen tree on the edge of the pond where she and Linnea hid during a twilight Sardines game last Fourth of July. We had searched and searched and had never been able to find them.

I feel a sense of anticipatory nostalgia. The afternoon glistens with such perfection that I already feel the missing. I want it to stay this way forever, this beautiful, this close—but the tide turns. All the talk of assessing ice and measuring risk has a subtext. Tara's body is filling out, boyfriends are starting to enter the scene, she feels the urge for adventure and separation. I feel I am preparing her metaphorically for the dark night on a city street when she needs to be attentive to cues in the landscape. Is it safe to proceed? I want her to be able to assess the risks of getting into a car driven by some guy she doesn't know after a party. We are rehearsing her departure.

In Our Wild Backyard

JANUARY 2, 2000.   It rained for of the first few days of the new millennium, and water began ponding on the ice. I was concerned that our ice forays would be thwarted, but I wasn't willing to give up that easily. Mindful of the Outward Bound saying, "There is no such thing as bad weather, just inappropriate clothing," I wanted to model persistence and stick-to-itiveness. I was also trying to treat staying at home for the holidays like being on vacation. When we go away, there's always energy for going on adventures, searching out new corners of the landscape. At home, it's easy to fall into habitual outings—the walk to the gorge or down to the Lion's Club field—the same old, same old. With no school and no work, we had the opportunity to be bold and strike out for new terrain. Even though I've lived in the Monadnock region for more than twenty-five years, it wouldn't take much to push beyond the familiar. And if we were on vacation, we wouldn't let a little drizzle slow us down.

Our neighbor Erin joined us. Tara recalls:

Today was quite a dreary day, but we decided we must go out for another adventure, because we hadn't been out for a whole two days. (Gasp!) We were slightly afraid that the rain had ruined the ice, and we prayed it would not start up again. Our first try, Chesham Pond, was horrible—in some places up to four inches of water on the ice. Our second destination, a little pond in Roxbury we'd never been to, was a little better, and the ice wasn't as mushy, so we concluded that small ponds might be better. I was ready to go home because it was getting late, but Daddy wanted to try Clapp Pond, another new one. I was getting bored with lacing, unlacing, and relacing my skates.

We followed a little trail down through the woods to a dark, narrow pond. By the time we had our skates on, it was almost 4:00 P.M., the light was dim, and the mist and fog were getting denser as the night set in. Too eerie for skating! Though covered with water in lots of places the ice was actually okay. After some time of what felt like floating two or three inches above the pond, we made it down to the outlet where we found the beaver lodge and food sticks stored by the beaver. We had to carefully tiptoe around on the thin ice. Erin and I felt shivers when we heard the ice crack, but no one fell in.

On the way up the pond on the other side, we discovered an old tree tipped over, with its root system sticking up out of the ice, maybe ten feet tall. All the dirt and earth that you usually see hanging from those things was gone, so it made an interweaving mazelike sculpture of old roots. Two of us would go behind it and stick our heads in the openings. Then the third person would get you to tilt your head sideways, or position it any way they pleased to make a strange, beheaded masterpiece. By that time it was almost dark and our feet were really wet and cold, so we headed back, periodically stopping to pop ice bubbles.

By sticking with the intent to skate every possible day and not being put off by the bad weather, we discovered a new species of experience—puddle skating. From Harrisville Pond and other outings, Tara had learned the diplomacy of thin ice, and trying out these sloppy, eerie conditions felt like the right next step. When we skated over ice covered with an inch of water, the darkened water made a reflective mirror surface and we could watch ourselves glide along—a visual first in all my fifty years. Although only a few miles from home, it felt as though we had stepped through the wardrobe into Narnia.

The previous spring, Tara had returned home from a multi-day school outing that included rock climbing and caving. The caving had been serious. They were underground for a number of hours, up to their waists in cold water, squirming through narrow passageways. The physical and psychic challenge had been just right for her at that point. She came home elated and struggled to explain her experience:

> I feel so enlightened, like a new self, like there's new parts of myself I discovered. I never knew I could do that stuff. You don't know even how to explore those places, and then chances come and you actually get to do it. It opens up a whole new world, like a cavern of darkness that someone has shone a light on. I knew I could bike and run, but I never knew how wild my world was, right here in my own backyard of New England.

Notice her analogy between light being shone on the darkness of the cavern and on unexplored parts of her self. The parallels between outward and inward explorations are particularly salient for adolescents.

Some Native American youths go wandering in the wilderness in search of a vision and a name, seeking to understand their personal gifts and their unique mission, striving to shed light on their inner lives. These skate explorations, encounters with ice in all forms, constitute my palette of personal wisdom. A tattooing of the soul. For Tara, I seek a kind of indelible, visceral knowledge of inner and outer places that will always be with her.

Feathers on Ice

JANUARY 8. It was the last weekend of school vacation, and we'd just returned from a couple of days' skiing. There was still no snow at home and the ice remained unblemished. I envisioned the consummation of all our preparations: the Nubanusit and Spoonwood loop. Nubanusit, the largest lake in our area, is deep, so it's often the last to freeze completely. You can start at the shallow end, skate a mile, and walk the portage trail to Spoonwood Pond, a protected wilderness pond. Next you skate the length of Spoonwood, clomp over the dam at the far end, and get back onto an arm of Nubanusit. Then it's out and around onto the wide, deep part of the lake and eventually, hopefully, back to the starting point.

Since Nubanusit rarely freezes completely before the snow flies, this five-mile skating loop is mostly a long-distance dream. In fact, I didn't know anybody who had done it. For Tara and me, this would be a quantum leap up. While our other forays had been outings of an hour or so, this was more of an expedition. Breaking through in marshy, shallow water is annoying but not really dangerous. Deep water, on the other hand, presents more of a life-and-death situation. And five miles requires endurance—of possible foot cramps, muscle fatigue, and, for me, back pain.

Tara understood the seriousness of what we were doing and made the commitment. She recalls:

> On this beautiful morning, we decided to attempt the loop around Nubanusit and Spoonwood, and the only thing stopping us from completing it would be the thickness of the ice. We got there, laced our skates and completed the first mile within fifteen minutes. The ice

was perfect for endless gliding and we both thought, "Well, this will be a shorter trip than we figured." We crossed the canoe trail on our skates, skating little frozen puddles on the way. As we started skating up Spoonwood, I felt this amazing sense of freedom. We had left behind the ice fishers and snowmobiles and now danced across the ice as if we were the only living creatures on this brisk, sunlit winter morning. As we got down toward the end of Spoonwood, we began to experience the first sections of thin ice. We avoided it, moving with care, but no real worry.

Well, not quite. Here's how I remember the rest of that day, interspersed with Tara's notes:

There's a big swath of open water to our left, at the end of the pond, with little wavelets kicking up in the wind. On the right there's a rocky peninsula with a channel of water between the ice and the shore. Between the two bands of open water is solid ice fifty feet wide, and we constantly check its thickness, but my pulse still surges as we tread lightly across the ice bridge. Here we're over deep water. We spread out and I go first, knowing that if the ice holds my weight, it will be okay for Tara. We talk about reasonable risk, and I suggest that we are starting to push against the edge. So we head for shore, take off our skates, and hike the last quarter mile until we're over the dam and onto a solidly frozen lobe of Nubanusit.

> TARA: As we move across Nubanusit again, we do start to get a little nervous, because the ice is thin and getting thinner. We inch along at the pace of a snail until it gets too thin to go any farther. It is about an inch thick, and that is nowhere near thick enough, so we decide to turn back.

Rounding the bend onto the wide part of Nubanusit, my skin starts to crawl. The ice is as black and smooth as a moonless night. And there's something spooky about the silence. I keep expecting to hear little hints of cracking, or that rolling thunder of ice expanding, but there's nothing. I wonder if the ice isn't even thick enough to make noise. We stay close to the shore, but the bottom drops off deeply here so it'll be full immersion if we go through. It's getting harder to check the ice depth visually, to see where the ice ends and the water begins, so I sit down to use the technique of kicking the rear end of my figure skate blade through the ice. One chop and water erupts through the fracture. The ice is barely an inch thick. I swallow gingerly and imagine creepy, anticipatory horror-movie music emerging from the crowded spruces along the shoreline, as if a shark is about to burst through the placid surface. Except that here the imagined music foreshadows that we are about to break through the placid ice into the frigid water below. Reluctantly we retreat, spacing ourselves widely over the half mile back to dependable ice. I'm happy to be free of those little shivers up and down my spine.

> TARA: We are both disappointed, but it does not mar the overall experience. We stop on the shore when we have about two miles to go. We build a little campfire, spread out a picnic, roast sausages and peppers, and eat while sunlight filters through the branches onto our faces. When we get back to the starting point and talk to the ice fishermen, they mention that the half of the loop we weren't able to skate is open water. It was definitely a good decision to turn back. We still ended up skating about five miles and it hardly felt like two. Skating is a wonderful way to travel. Too bad Venice isn't a city on ice.

At lunch, we stretch out in the leaves, an odd combination of January temperatures and October dryness. I talk to Tara about "the wisdom of not doing," Freeman Tilden's term for projects better left undone. On Harrisville Pond, it was right to take the risk and keep going, to honor the original intent and thus make it far up into the marshy interior. Courage is good. Today it was right to turn back. Humility is good. For everything there is a season. I hope Tara will store these memories of ice as guideposts for future dilemmas. Should I take this job, should I stay up all night to finish this assignment, should I trust this guy? She is developing the skills to make those decisions.

Carefree, we stride back up the expanse of Spoonwood, leaving long, symmetrical blade marks on the slate surface. At the peninsula where

Tara and I camped for a couple of nights three or four years ago, we recall the good diving spots, the time we drew sketches of the canoe in the
late afternoon light, and the hike over to Elephant Rock where we stuffed
our mouths chipmunk-full of blueberries. A bit farther on, we stop at a
trail of feathers, wind-drifted as far as the eye can follow. The remnants
of a grouse taken by a coyote, perhaps. Each downy feather frozen delicately on a satin backdrop, like our string of skating afternoons.

Fire and Ice

A couple of weeks after that magic day, I dropped Tara off at Yankee
Lanes to meet Colin for her first real date. Our last planned ski day that
winter didn't work out because Tara wanted to go snowboarding with
friends. Just in the past few months, we'd started to talk about needing
a second phone line because Tara was talking to her friends endlessly.
Irony and eye shadow were becoming more common on her face. She
wasn't around on weekends as much, and we were all starting to miss her
a bit. But she was incredibly helpful around the house, she could make
a mean guacamole, and it had become really enjoyable to talk to her
about presidential politics and the morality of environmental pollution.
She was growing up.

Wendy and I considered it valuable to mark each new developmental
shift our children made. Our goals for Tara's transition into adolescence
were to honor the child she'd been, celebrate the person she was becoming, and, if possible, pass on some wisdom about right livelihood. We recognized that she was developing her own set of values and moral principles, and thought she should have good models of other adults who were
bonded to the natural world. So when she was fourteen, we encouraged
Tara to participate in a Girl's Coming of Age program offered by Kroka
Expeditions—six girls and two women leaders tucked into an isolated
campsite near a lake in the Green Mountain wilderness for a week.

Together the girls and leaders created a different ritual experience
each day. On a frame of saplings they wove stick-and-reed walls that
became a Moon Lodge, where they learned the importance of giving and

receiving. Another day they immersed themselves in the mud and muck of a bog, allowed the slime to harden on their skins, and then walked half a mile to wash off in the cool waters of the clear lake. The grime and refreshment of adult life. One late afternoon they huddled under a tarp on top of their life preservers as a violent microburst thunderstorm ripped across southern Vermont and New Hampshire. As I sat in my office in the odd green light and torrents of rain fell outside, I felt pangs of anxiety and the mixed sadness and joy of her independence.

At the start of the week, the leaders had each girl and parent hold opposite ends of a length of yarn to signify their connections. Then the yarn was snipped: a symbol of separation. The parents were to bring back their pieces of yarn at the journey's end. Throughout the week, the girls endured hardship yet were nurtured by the leaders and each other. On their last night they did a traditional sweat ritual, "one of the hardest things I've ever done," Tara said later. They talked about who they had been as children, who they were becoming, and what they had learned from their parents. At the ceremonial reentry, their laughter and stories let us parents glimpse the community of young womanhood that had emerged during the week. The girls had taken the thread of connection with their parents and woven it into something beautiful, like the designs they had woven with their strands of yarn.

All the girls kept journals during the week. In her final entry, Tara wrote:

> Looking up at the sky through the foliage, I realize that my life is a truly precious and beautiful thing. I want to kindle its spark, bring it to flame, and, if I can, bring it to a roaring fire of happiness. Which will not be stomped out or extinguished in any unnatural way, so that it may burn down to the last ember, which will then quietly, happily slip into the blissful and endless sleep of Death.

All our encounters with ice and its kin—exploratory skating, cold-water immersions, difficult skiing—paradoxically helped kindle Tara's spark. The harsh coldness outside necessitates a fire of inner determination. The steep slope makes muscles burn. Facing death means embracing life. I believe that Tara's fire was stoked by her memories of "dancing across the ice as if we were the only living creatures on that brisk, sunlit winter morning."

Doing Tuckerman's
Rites of Passage at the Right Time

Stroll from the harbor in Portland, Maine—down where the big car ferries depart for Nova Scotia—up to the Western Promenade, a serene urban park with a great view. Look northwest. On a clear day, Mount Washington and the Presidential Range in New Hampshire's White Mountains loom unexpectedly. High peaks so close to the sea-weedy, seagulled shore? Especially in autumn or late spring, when winter is a vague anticipation or a receding memory, the snow-covered peaks glow eerily, like a recurrent dream you can't forget.

Tuckerman's Ravine, an ultra-steep, snowy bowl high on the flanks of Mount Washington, looms similarly in a young northern New England skier's consciousness. If you've grown up downhill skiing every weekend and vacation—so dedicated that you'll leave the house in pitch darkness at 5:30 A.M., when it's sixteen degrees below zero, so you can be sure to get first tracks—then Tuckerman's is an inevitability, a calling at the dawn of adolescence. That was Eli.

I hadn't skied as a child and then only a few times in high school, so I always felt a bit intimidated on skis. But when I heard a friend comment, "Learning to ski gave me a deep sense of centeredness, an irrefutable balance and self-confidence, a calmness in the face of risk, that I have carried into all other aspects of my life," I decided we would be a skiing family. We started when Tara was six and Eli four, spending lots of afternoons on the rope tow at dinky Temple Mountain. I'd have one of the kids on a strap out in front of me, or sometimes holding onto my outstretched ski pole. We did the same boring slope over and over until things fell into place.

Over the next six or seven years, Eli, Tara, and I became serious skiers. I have many concerns about the environmental ethics of ski resorts, about the impacts of snow making, stream reductions, massive sewage treatment, and habitat fragmentation. (And I'm cheered by the recent Green Slopes movement to make ski area operation more sustainable.) But regardless of the downside, for me and my kids it was worth it. We loved the camaraderie of early departures, weird conditions, and virgin corduroy. Even through the summer we would talk fondly of memorable slopes—of the fresh powder on Mythmaker that day at Attitash, the impossible death cookies on that ungroomed slope at Killington, the time we mastered bumps on an empty Tuesday at Haystack.

When Tara was eleven, she came back from an after-school ski day with her friends and volunteered, "I'm so happy you taught me how to ski, Daddy, because it's really given me self-confidence. I can get past being afraid now because I know how to face risks calmly and not get overwhelmed." I was pleased as punch.

By the time Eli was ten, he was a hot skier, always seeking out the twisty side trails, the natural and kid-made jumps on the edges of the groomed slopes. He joined the freestyle team at Mount Sunapee and began to channel his wild energy into refined mogul and trick skiing. Some days I'd ski all day and never see him, and he'd come back with stories of fifteen-foot cliffs, secret glades, stashes of powder. Or he'd be in the park all afternoon working on 540s, iron tails, and barrel rolls. I remember riding the North Peak Triple at Sunapee one day and there he was, training bumps on Flying Goose. He was skiing by himself, unaware that I was watching. His easy rhythm, his gracefulness, his ability to make an impossible slope look like a walk on the beach brought tears of joy to my eyes.

The next couple of winters, we tromped around northern New England on the competition circuit. When not competing, Eli challenged himself on some of the hardest slopes in New England: Ovation and Devil's Fiddle at Killington, White Heat at Sunday River, Castlerock at Sugarbush. And he started to bug me about Tuckerman's. "Peter's dad skied it when he was twelve! I'm ready. Can't we do it?" he'd plead. But though I thought he might be good enough, I wasn't really sure I was ready to let him go.

To put him to the test, I arranged an outing to Jay Peak, New England's true dyed-in-the-wool skier destination, where you can ski glades, bumps, and steeps for days and not take the same trail twice. I skied way beyond my ability and tumbled down a gruesome slope called Green Beret. Eli couldn't get enough. One morning I hitched him up with Dieter, a gaunt old German instructor with a steely demeanor, and told him to really challenge Eli. They skied Valhalla, one of the steeper glades on the mountain, and Eli wanted more. As we rode the gondola up over the summit cone, I agreed to let him ski The Face by himself, the gnarliest combination of krummholtz (twisted, wind-stunted spruce), ledge drops, and exposure in northern New England skiing, at least in-bounds. It's the venue for one of Vermont's few extreme skiing competitions. I knew I couldn't ski it, but I was reasonably sure that he had the necessary skills. I had to trust him and let him go. When he popped out of the woods at the bottom with a big smile on his face, I knew he was ready for Tuckerman's.

My strategy during Eli and Tara's adolescent development was to help them find the right kinds of challenges at the right stages for their unique personalities. In traditional cultures the rite of passage is often an encounter with wildness that includes arduous physical endeavors, a confrontation with solitude, and some harsh education about the interpenetration of life and death. These experiences test the young person's mettle and help him move from carefree childhood into responsible adulthood. Without real challenges shaped and monitored by thoughtful adults, teenagers create their own dangerous rites: they may drive fast, use drugs and alcohol in excess, join gangs, play with sex. By engaging them in appropriate challenges that balance real edginess with reasonable checks and balances, we can, with luck, move them through this identity-defining and risk-taking phase with their bodies and souls intact and invigorated.

I knew that Tuckerman's was the right next step for Eli. It would have been easy to slough it off: too much effort, too busy a time of year, concerns about my physical fitness—these were all available reasons for not bothering. But I knew I needed to honor the right time–right place principle. He was thirteen, it had been a reasonably good snow year, and my colleague Bo was an experienced Tuckerman's skier. I had to seize the season.

Uphill Climb

I make the arrangements with Bo, our trusty guide, a month in advance, but I don't tell Eli. Partly because I want to reserve the opportunity to wimp out, partly because I want it to be a surprise. A few days before T-day, I let him in on the plan. He's thrilled and nervous. We drive up the night before, stopping to eat at Horsefeathers in North Conway, a favorite destination of rock climbers and mountaineers. Over dinner I explain the glacial geography of the ravine and the meteorological reasons for Tuckerman's getting so much snow.

We stay at Laurie Jean's house in Jackson. She helps organize the annual bike race up Mount Washington and had competed in the running race up the auto road the year before. She's a role model of an adult who takes on serious physical challenges. My choices are conscious: I'm using the heightened awareness evoked by Eli's excitement to educate him about the mountain environment and how people use the mountains for inspiration and personal growth.

That night, after a week of premature summer and perfect spring skiing, an arctic high barrels in. When we roll out of bed early, it's about ten degrees with a sharp wind from the northwest. In my mind's eye I see all that soft pliable corn snow transformed into convoluted concrete. But when the snow gets tough, the tough go skiing. We meet Bo and John, a sixteen-year-old who has already been initiated, in the wind-whipped parking lot at the Appalachian Mountain Club lodge. Skiers are busy strapping their skis to their packs and slapping on zinc oxide. A run down Tuckerman's isn't cheaply bought for the price of a lift ticket; you have to hike up to Hermit Lake Shelter and then into the bowl, a steep three and a half miles with a vertical gain of about 3,000 feet.

Eli describes the beginning of the trip:

> It was late April when my dad and I arrived at Pinkham Notch Camp. The whole last week had been warm and seventy degrees and then, of course, the weather turned bad when we arrived. But that didn't stop us or the other hard-core skiers and snowboarders who arrived. After gearing up and spending a few moments in the gift shop looking at White Mountain guides and Tuckerman's bumper stickers, we headed off. It was cold, but by the first bridge (about two-tenths of a mile up the trail) I was stripping layers off so that all I had on was some polypro and a vest. My shoulders started to ache but my mind started to think. I couldn't wait to see that first view of Tucks. Hiking up the trail felt like a transition from my boyhood to teenagerhood.

Eli and I have done lots of camping but not a lot of backpacking, and I know this hike will be significantly harder than anything he's done before. He has his skis, boots, lots of warm clothes, water, and lunch in his pack, which weighs about thirty pounds. In the past Eli has shown a low threshold for uphill trudging, and I am concerned that complaining will kick in not very far up the trail. But a combination of factors works to create positive momentum. First of all, we are with an older teenager who sets the pace and the emotional style. John is good-spirited, committed, and steady. Having a slightly older role model compels Eli to rise to the occasion. Second, the camaraderie of all the skiers ascending, and the fact that we often pass other groups of teens, makes Eli feel like a tough little dude. When he is just with me, I see him fray around the edges and get near tears, but the constant presence of a trail audience works to contain his emotions. He is being pushed, but pushed within his available limits.

After a brief gorp break at Hermit Lake shelter amid a sea of Gore-Tex, long hair, and balaclavas, we start up over the little headwall into the base of the ravine. The trail gets narrow and steep as you climb out of the forest and move toward your first glimpse of the day's challenge. Eli describes:

> As we neared the base of the bowl we came around the corner, and there was the headwall looming up like a giant. The mother of all ski runs in New England, and I was standing at the base of it. I felt proud of myself, but then my stomach felt like I had just gotten off a roller coaster. I was in a mixed emotional state of excitement, worriedness, and awe.

Just before the steep pitch up the little headwall (a hint of the monster headwall ahead), we take a breather and Bo tells a story I have heard only snatches of before:

> Listen to this, Eli. It was right about here, a couple of years ago. Lots more snow and it was really warm, so there was a big meltwater stream coming over the little headwall, flowing right down below us there, then disappearing into a tunnel underneath the ice and snow pack. Just as I came over this lip, I could hear someone screaming, and I look down. There's a girl partially submerged in the stream. She wasn't much older than you, Eli. She must have slipped off the trail and tumbled down into the water. She's in the current and barely holding on to a rock, and she's about fifty feet from where the stream disappears under the snow. If she gets pulled down that tunnel, she's dead.
>
> I'm alone, my friends are both ahead of me and behind me, so I have no choice. I drop my pack, glissade down the slope into the stream and grab onto her. Seems like she was just about to give up when I got there. I've got her, but then I realize there's no way I can get both her and myself out of the stream. If I free my hands to climb, I've got to let go of her. So I start to yell. Luckily a couple more skiers hear us and come down and pull us both out. If I hadn't come along at just the right moment, she would have been history. Only time I clearly saved someone's life. So don't let your guard down, Eli. Tuckerman's is a dangerous place.

As the story proceeds, I watch Eli's eyes getting wider and wider. I can see he understands that we are playing for keeps.

Next stop is Lunch Rocks, a jumble of boulders at the base of the headwall that serves as a staging area. Here you dump your gear, put on ski boots, figure out how you want to carry your skis, and start the serious climbing, inching your way as far up the slope as you want to ski down. I labor up about 300 feet and figure that's far enough for me, thank you. "Oh, come on, Daddy! You're not going to stop here, are you?"

The real skiers continue on up another 300 feet or so. But with the clarity that comes with advanced age and the recognition that this was not a test of *my* mettle, I put on my skis on a tiny little platform above a rock and stumble my way down, taking three or four turns. I feel completely happy that I can now say I've skied Tuckerman's.

Playing for Keeps

Then I hunker down into a wind-protected spot to watch Eli. He describes:

> We climbed up to the base of the runs and we started to hike up Right Chute for our first run. The condition of the snow couldn't have been worse, but skiing was only part of this experience. We reached about halfway up Right Chute and decided that would be far enough to take a run. The first run down was harder than I expected. It was like when you look at a bump run from the chairlift. It always looks easier from the lift than it actually is. Well, looking at this from the bottom looked fine, but coming down was a lot different. Little snowslides would start, ice chunks would roll by, but I made it down safe and almost sound.

Actually, quite sound. Eli looks as competent as anyone else that day, even though he is one of the youngest skiers out there. I'm proud of him.

We bundle up, eat lunch, gawk at the spectacle of clouds rushing over the rim of the headwall against the sunglass-enhanced cobalt blue ski, and pick out tiny skiers inching their way up the other side of the bowl. We get stiffly cold, and then Bo motivates the boys for one more run. I'm content to supervise.

This time they climb a long, long way up to a tiny ledge below an immense boulder. Mason, a slightly older neighbor of ours, took a long fall on Hillman's Highway on the other side of the bowl last winter, hobbled around for months afterward, and still has scars to show for it. I cross my fingers and pray that Eli is protected by higher forces.

The second run was way scarier than the first. I snapped in, put my skis over the edge of the little lip we were sitting on, and looked down. It kind of freaked me out, my heart was racing, but I knew I had to go. The start was hardest, a long drop down a fifty-degree slope, but once I'd made a couple of turns I knew I could do it and I relaxed. It didn't take a lot of skill, just a lot of guts, and lots of little jump turns.

Only two runs, skiers may wonder? But it's cold, it's a long hike down, and you can barely imagine how much energy hiking the headwall takes out of you. We're ready to roll, so we pack up and ski from Lunch Rocks down to the bottom edge of the bowl where the trail enters the woods. Sitting on a rock as we change boots, we gaze back up into the fullness of the cirque. Bo calls our attention to a tiny speck way up high on the mountain. "Hey, look up there, on the slope above the headwall!"

In the absolute center of the bowl, above the rocky cliffs poking out of the snow, above the steepest part of the headwall, is a snowboarder heading for the edge of the world. My knee-jerk selfish thought is, "I really don't want to have to be part of a rescue operation." We watch slack-jawed as he starts down, takes two or three turns, spills, and tumbles over a cliff—about a thirty- or forty-foot fall, crashing through shrubs, careening off rocks, down to a jutting-out ledge but still way up the headwall. Then nothing, no movement. I'm sure we just watched this guy die. And nobody else saw it happen.

"Aren't we going to do something?" Eli pleads. We don't have much choice. At the base of the Lunch Rocks is a ski patrol encampment—three or four guys who hike up each day from Hermit Lake to assess avalanche risk, provide first aid, conduct evacuations. We are fairly sure they couldn't have seen the fall, and it is our responsibility to inform them. We trudge the quarter mile back up to their station and report in. Scanning the cliffs with high-powered binoculars, we finally pick out where he is, lying in an unmoving heap. Wait, is that a glimmer of movement or just the wind moving some branches? The ski patrollers are remarkably blasé about the event.

"Aren't you guys going to mount an evacuation effort? It was a pretty bad fall," I insist.

"Do you have any idea how long and hard it is to get up there?" one of them responds. "And besides, yesterday three guys did exactly the same thing, and they all walked away. We're going to give him some time before we move out."

Sure enough, over the next ten minutes, the boarder starts to move around, then he looks like he's sitting up, and then: What's that, a puff of smoke? He's having a cigarette—or something. We figure we've fulfilled our responsibility and retreat. By the time we make it back to our gear, it looks as though he is sliding down off the ledge to get to a place where he can start riding again. And when a scruffy, overalled, and dreadlocked boarder passes us as we descend, really hoofing it, we realize it's him, resurrected from the near dead. Another story to enhance the mystique of Tucks.

It's a long laborious trip down. Next time, we agree, we'll come early enough to ski the Sherburne Trail, which allows you to ski from Hermit Lake Shelter all the way back down to Pinkham Notch when there's enough snow. No more hiking both up *and* down. But Eli is garrulous the whole way; he and John have hit it off and talk about school and skiing. Bo and I talk work and relationships. We all bask in the glow of accomplishment. When I overhear Eli say, "I can't wait to get back to school and brag about my expedition with my dad," I feel completely fulfilled. At Pinkham we weigh our packs and grab some junk food, and though it's an exorbitant $17, I buy Eli the T-shirt that bears the motto "Sometimes the road to the stars isn't a road at all."

When I asked him, about a year later, if skiing Tuckerman's changed him at all, Eli summarized the experience well:

It was always something I wanted to do when I was younger, like it was the guy thing to do. So I felt I had really done something big, like I had conquered it. And, mentally, I think it made me a better skier, since it helped me manage my fear. Last summer when I hiked up to Carter Notch and when I hiked those peaks around Zealand with my class, I used that same backpack Bo lent me. When I'd start to feel tired I'd think, well, this backpack went up Tuckerman's and this isn't nearly as hard, so I knew I could do it. After Tuckerman's, I knew I could be more adventurous and take on bigger challenges, because I knew I was strong.

There were other passages for Eli during adolescence—first girlfriends, mountain biking in Utah, designing and producing his first ski video, his first top-three finish in a freestyle event. But I think doing Tucks was his big stride from boyhood into teenagerhood, and one of his first times he consciously recognized his own inner strength.

The Door in the Rock
Canyoneering in Zion

rriving at 7:20 A.M., with early summer hotness just starting to simmer toward the predicted high of 101 degrees, Tara and I already feel late. The prep room at Zion Adventures is humming with logistical preparations.

Guide Tamara engages us quickly. "Here's your canyon pack and dry bag. Unload it. Should be fleece tops and bottoms, a drysuit, your harness, and a sling of 'biners [carabiners]. Try on these neoprene socks and stream shoes; see if they fit. Throw in your water and food. We're trying to pull out in about fifteen minutes."

The core mission of Zion Adventures' training is to prepare adventure seekers with the skills to do canyoneering descents in the wide array of daunting slot canyons throughout Zion National Park and southwestern Utah. A relatively new sport, canyoneering involves traveling in canyons that require technical descents with harnesses, ropes, and full-water immersion gear for wet descents and swimming. It is most often practiced in narrow gorges with numerous drops, sculptured walls, and spectacular waterfalls. Because Zion is the last national park that does not allow commercial guiding, Zion Adventures must conduct its trainings outside the park boundaries. Once people have demonstrated their competence, the company provides equipment, technical advice, and shuttles for explorers to take on the Virgin Narrows, the Subway, Orderville, Keyhole, Echo, and other progressively harder canyon descents.

Two days ago we hiked and swam Clear Creek Canyon, and yesterday we scrambled up one of the Northgate Peaks. Today we've signed on to learn canyoneering in Water Canyon, about twenty back-road miles south of Zion Adventures' outfitting center. We'll be rappelling down waterfalls fed by melting snowpack into shadowed canyon pools, narrow as slivers—hence the fleece and drysuit in spite of the summer heat.

There are two leaders and six canyoneers-in-training: four women plus eighteen-year-old Tara and myself. The women have just been climbing at Red Rocks in Nevada; they do a climbing trip each spring. Maria, their leader, is taut and spindly, scuffed and tough. "We call her Spider Woman," says her friend Ondi, "because she just sticks to the wall. Climbs 5.11s, has no fear." Gulp. The hardest technical climbs are rated about 5.14, so 5.11 is hard. I haven't climbed technically in twenty years—even then never anything harder than a 5.8—and I can barely remember how to rappel. Tara's had only minimal climbing and rappelling experience. These ladies sound like crackerjacks; I wonder if Tara and I are in over our heads.

We load the Toyota Land Cruiser, squash all eight of us inside, and head west, then south on a steep, twisty, deeply rutted dirt road toward Hilldale, Utah, on the Arizona border. I have that mixed excited-anxious feeling that I often get before a new challenge. But mostly I am thrilled to be perched on the threshold of a door that I saw in my mind's eye more than a decade earlier.

Equally as Bold

This trip had numerous purposes. Tara and I had been to Utah the preceding year, when I served on the advisory board for a National Science

Foundation grant for the Four Corners School of Outdoor Education in Monticello, Utah. The board meeting took place during a four-day raft trip on the San Juan River. It had been too short. Tara and I loved the rafting, and we'd both gotten particularly intrigued with the side canyons that we never had enough time to explore.

Furthermore, I hadn't seen her in more than four months. By the time Tara was approaching her senior year of high school, she was ready for a change. Academically sophisticated, she felt unchallenged, even though she was taking AP Environmental Studies and some other courses at the local college. This had given her a taste of academic freedom and community activism, which was more her style. She was ready to stop being a passive learner and to start actively giving back and learning on her own.

So for the second half of her senior year, she went off to Monteverde, Costa Rica, to do a teaching internship program at the Cloud Forest School. Based on the principles of sustaining the ecological and cultural integrity of the Costa Rican cloud forest ecosystem, the school provides bilingual education for mostly local children. Though the internship was designed for college graduates, we figured Tara was mature enough to take advantage of the opportunity. The whole experience, working at the school as well as traveling on her own, had been a rollicking adventure featuring scorpions, classroom management challenges, and surfing big waves. She witnessed a guns-a-blazing bank robbery in Monteverde, visited an isolated Panamanian archipelago, and had a minor brush with the law.

She arrived home only a few weeks before we were due to depart for another of my Utah board meetings. I looked forward to this trip as an opportunity to debrief her about her travels in leisurely fashion, but I also wanted to make sure that it was edgy enough to be a memorable rite of passage for her. Her Costa Rica sojourn had been a true seeking-a-vision-in-the-wilderness opportunity. She was clearly on her way to being her own woman. This Utah excursion had to be equally as bold, an adventure that would challenge us as coequals and move us along in the transition from father and daughter to colleagues or friends—whatever you call a close and respectful relationship between parents and adult children. Canyoneering would be new and equally challenging for both of us, since I could fall prey to vertigo as easily as she.

Reading through my journals in preparing for the trip, I realized that there was also an odd kind of predestination to it. In my description of Tara's first hike up a real mountain, southern New Hampshire's Gap Mountain, when she was five years old, I found this passage:

On the blueberry ledges on top, we have a picnic and I tell her a story about a daddy and a little girl and a bunny who climb a mountain. While the daddy naps, the little girl and the bunny find a door in a rock that leads underground to a cavern with a grotto of sparkling gems. They take some gems in exchange for some gifts they leave behind.

As soon as I finish the story, Tara jumps up to go look for the door in the rock. Oops! I was intending the story to focus us on finding beautiful pieces of quartz, but she's not the least bit interested in quartz anymore. She wants to find the door. Even when I suggest that maybe the story isn't about *this* mountain, she wants to search and search. She gets it in her head that the door will be in a small overhanging ledge cave that we saw on the way up. She pushes me to start going down and to keep moving until we get there. She's significantly disappointed when we find the cave but don't find the door. But I tickle her and we run down the mountain until her spirits are lifted.

I realize that this story stuff may be a little problematic. Perhaps I'm creating expectations that lead to disappointment and sadness. But then I remember a story I've heard about a secret cabin built into the cliff on Mount Monadnock. A door in the rock. I tell Tara, and she wants to climb Monadnock right now. Some other day, I promise.

Still focusing on doorways in rocks, I think of mausoleums, the Anasazi ruins at Mesa Verde, Chaco Canyon, and Hovenweep—places I have always wanted to visit. I get images of the passageways in the pyramids. Maybe the door in the rock is the seed of a new story waiting to happen.

Descending Water Canyon

And now here we are, in the landscape of Anasazi ruins, opening literal and figurative doors in rocks. A few days earlier we'd been squeezing into rock ruins in the side canyons along the San Juan River. Now we'll be descending into slot canyons, the hidden passageways to treasure grottos. Canyoneering is a way to open the door. We're following a path that we imagined long ago.

Which all sounds rather charming but like a lot of hooey now that we're perched on the edge of the first rappel, a descent via a fixed rope down a vertical canyon wall occupied mostly by a waterfall. The slot canyon we're going to follow is carved by the stream that tumbles down it. Since the canyon is often only as wide as the stream, we'll mostly be rappelling in waterfalls, or swimming canyon pools, or scrambling along sculptured sandstone in between these water features. We've squirmed our way into drysuits because once we drop off the edge, the inner canyon temperature will be twenty degrees cooler and the water temperature will be downright cold.

The rappel rope runs through a carabiner secured by webbing to a stable tree. It's apparent that, with very little instruction, we're expected to back off this cliff and rappel down to a ledge that is halfway down the eighty-foot waterfall.

The other four women seem to know exactly what's going on. There's a stream of sweat running down my arm inside the drysuit, a combination of the heat and my high anxiety. Tara's face wears that squinty, what-have-you-gotten-me-into look. Later she recalls, "I didn't want to say anything, but I was so scared I was about to cry." This from a girl with a high tolerance for risk. But we were both too wussy to confess our fear, and so first she, then I, walked off the cliff.

The hardest part, as they say, is trusting the equipment. Of course, you intuitively want to stay close to the cliff, but then you've got no traction. It's best when you get your legs perpendicular to the cliff, so you've got to lean away from the rock, letting your backside lead you down. Down to a tiny little midstream rock platform, three or four feet wide, a tendril of stream, and the guide and you scrunched together as if you were getting on a subway train at rush hour. You click into the safety loop, disengage from the first rope, run the second rope through a special fitting on the harness around your waist, tie your autoblock (a backup knot), then delink from the safety. This time you rappel—the waterfall flowing between your legs—down into the waist-deep frigid pool. Tara and I have to learn all these techniques very quickly and very well to protect ourselves from imminent demise.

Tara is sitting on the sandbar with a full-moon grin on her face as I come down. "Way to go, Daddy!" I look around. Cliff walls soar upward into a cobalt blue sky. The waterfall splatters playfully into a deep pool edged with a honey sand beach. The only way out is through a four-foot wide crack that soon leads to another forty-foot waterfall. Like Alice, we've dropped into the rabbit hole.

Soon we're at the crest of the next waterfall descent. Guide Evan tosses the rope bags down to the pool at the bottom. "This time we're going to practice down-climbing, which means working your way down the face with no equipment. Don't worry, it looks way harder than it actually is." Which is good to hear because it looks very hard. The pitch is not vertical but rather fifty or sixty degrees. You've got to sit in the stream, wedge yourself into the crack, and pick your way down to a bit of a ledge, then squirm underneath a big boulder and down another crack, into the pool below.

Spiderwoman, sticks-like-glue-to-vertical-faces Maria, breezily volunteers to go first. Five feet into the descent, she freaks. "I can't do it! I can't do it! I just don't feel secure on this wet rock. I don't know where to put my feet." She climbs back up to the start. Guide Tamara assures her that it's an easy puzzle to work out. She encourages Maria to take deep breaths, points out hand- and footholds, suggests jamming her butt into the crack for friction, assures her that she's got all the time in the world. What's supposed to be a quick descent takes her a grueling fifteen minutes.

Tara and I look at each other and wordlessly concur, "Holy shit! She's by far the best climber in the group, she's fearless, and she's freaking out.

We're going to die." I can already hear the *thwop, thwop, thwop* of the medevac helicopter coming in.

Maria makes it down, and thankfully the next couple of women descend with comparative ease. As Tara's about to start her descent, I say my ritualistic good-byes, as on a midnight flight with Eli the previous February, coming into Boston in a snowstorm. We pulled out of our approach at the last minute because they had to close the runway for snow removal and ice treatment. Listening to the flight-control patter, I had discerned that the pilot on a flight just ahead of us had found the braking on the snow-covered runway "fair to poor." As they cleared us for landing, I turned to Eli, told him how much I loved him, said it had been a privilege being his dad.

And here I am again, saying the same thing to Tara. It turns out I do worry too much. Tara makes it look doable, and I pretty much scamper down. Long legs help, and those stream shoes are remarkably sticky, even on wet rock.

At the end of the day, Tara and I are asked to set up the final rappel with only minimal help from a guide. There's a fixed bolt to run the rope through, and it's only about a thirty-foot drop. No stream to contend with. Putting our heads together, we figure it out relatively easily, and then I have to rappel first—the proof of the pudding. Applying everything I've learned, I clip in, move across the ledge to find the fall line so I don't pendulum when I go over the edge, and slip down gracefully. Tara follows with similar aplomb.

She and I are starting to look like seasoned apprentices. But as we extract ourselves from the restrictive drysuits, reorganize our climbing gear, and slug down pints of water, I query, "Think we're ready to try this ourselves?"

"No way!" she replies. I completely agree with her.

Lamb Knoll

The next day, it's just Tara and I with Jonathan, the founder of Zion Adventures. He's been spoken of in hushed, reverential terms by all the other staff. The plan is to meet him at Lamb Knoll, serendipitously just a half-mile walk from where we're staying.

Our domicile for the week is a funky, off-the-grid, solar-powered, handmade home in Cave Valley, way out on the Kolob Plateau road 11.3 miles north of Virgin, Utah. It belongs to a friend of mine who is off traveling, so we have it to ourselves. The road passes through the park for a long ways, then onto private land for a mile or so, through a beautiful vale of verdant rangeland surrounded by peaks and sculptured sandstone ridges. The isolated house is tucked into a copse of oak trees in the middle of a sweep of meadows, looking out onto the Ridge of 100 Peaks, the North and South Guardian Angels, Tabernacle Dome, and Cave Knoll. The previous owner was a sculptor, so there's artwork scattered throughout the landscape—steel steeds, ornate gateways, graveyards of stone, birds frozen in flight. There are plenty of live beasts too: Cave Valley is fecund mountain lion terrain. The only documented attack on a person in Zion happened up the road a couple of miles, and in the chaparral across the way are the rotting remains of a cow brought down by a lion. Makes you think twice about going for a solo twilight walk.

We stroll down the road and wait for Jonathan at a pull-off just where the paved road exits the park into Cave Valley. We've been told we'll be descending a couple of dry "super slots," and nervous anticipation is creeping back into our throats. While we're waiting for Jonathan's truck to pull in, he appears instead walking down the range road from Lamb Knoll, an upthrust mesa of sandstone. We chat pleasantly for a few minutes and are soothed by his assured demeanor. I can feel his years of climbing big walls and his grit in the face of extreme exposure, forged into a palpable Zen patience. This is a guy you feel comfortable entrusting your life to.

Setting off, we scramble up dry washes, through scrub oak thickets and then onto slickrock: sensuous but sometimes crumbly sandstone. As the steepness increases, Tara and I get more anxious. When Jonathan points out the route up and around the next hoodoo, a pinnacle of rock on the ridge we're ascending, I say, "Well, if was up to me, I wouldn't try this, but I'm assuming you've assessed our chicken-ness in relation to our competence level, and have determined we can do this."

"Yup," he tosses back. "I'm familiar with all kinds of chicken—buffalo wings, dark meat, plump white meat breasts. I've tasted it all, and I've assessed your level. I make a point of doing something outside of my comfort zone every day. And even though this is outside of your comfort zone, I know you can do it."

And he's right. We top out to a view that stretches from Saint George in the southwestern corner of the state to the ragged Pine Ridge Mountains to the 10,000-foot mesas up toward Cedar Breaks to the north—the source of all the frigid snowmelt flowing down through the bone-dry canyons of Zion. Then we descend through open bowls to our first canyon. "Ancient slots," Jonathan describes. "Water hasn't flowed through here in thousands of years. These were probably formed after the last ice age. Very different from Water Canyon."

Thankfully the first couple of rappels are easy. After we inspect the belay anchors, Jonathan assumes we know what we're doing. He thoughtfully lets us reconstruct our learning from yesterday, and with little coaching we remember the complicated sequence of carabiner attachments, knots, safety checks. Piece of cake, we feel after the second descent.

The third rappel is short but odd. The initial crack is barely shoulder width, and you have to wiggle laboriously to make backward progress. Then there's an awkward transition onto a down-sloping log. There's no place to put an anchor, so Jonathan serves as the fixed point for the rope. If there's a fall, it's his weight and strength we'll be depending on. I manage a relatively easy descent. Tara follows, and right before my eyes, at the transition, she falls, pivots upside down, smacks against the cliff, and is barely stopped by her autoblock, with her head only about four feet above the ground.

I help her unravel and lower herself to the wash bottom. "I'm okay, I'm okay," she assures me, but she's visibly shaken. Once Jonathan climbs down to us, he takes her hand in his and watches carefully. "A bit of jitters, but once the adrenaline wears off, you'll be fine." We slither out the bottom of the canyon and he asks if we're up for a second descent. Bravely, Tara agrees, ready to get back on the horse.

Over lunch, sitting in a shady alcove at the top of the next rappel, we share deeply personal stories. Tucked inaccessibly into serpentine enfoldments, living on the edge, it is as if we have entered into dreamtime. The quality of the moment feels like an initiation rite in which we can all risk openness, and the stories help take Tara away from her recent scare.

The next chasm beckons. A long drop—80 feet or so, Jonathan indicates. Long enough to require that we securely link our 110- and 85-foot ropes together with a fisherman's knot so we can be rappelling on two ropes, an added safety precaution. When I ask how this compares to the other descents, Jonathan suggests it isn't much different from anything we have already done. If I'd known the truth, I probably would have balked.

Regrettably for Tara, this one starts just like the one she fell on earlier. A tight beginning and then an awkward transition. Except this time there is much more verticality and exposure; looking out from the top, we can't see anything beyond the first eight or ten feet. We have literally no idea what we're dropping into. It looks like the edge of the world. Being the good dad, I volunteer to go first and discover that it's much harder than anything we've done. The tightness of the beginning crack makes inching backward feel like a breech birth. My right hand is so crammed between the rock and my thigh that I have to abrade the back of my hand to move my autoblock down the rope. Lactic acid building up in my muscles starts to cause the uncontrollable vibration climbers refer to as sewing machine legs. I'm finally able to extract myself from the crack and get onto the wall, where the going is easier.

About two-thirds of the way down, I glance over my shoulder to see the rope bag at the end of one of my ropes dangling against the cliff just below me, not resting comfortably on the ground where it should be. In other words, I'm at the end of one of my ropes. Did Jonathan make a mistake? Or did he plan this so I'd have to problem-solve in midclimb? I'm in a pickle. Luckily there's a bit of a ledge at my feet where I can rest so that not all my weight is on the rope. "I'm out of rope on one side," I yell up to Jonathan.

There are a few moments of silence as he assesses the problem. I see him visualizing the situation, conceptualizing how he's going to support me as I make the necessary modifications. I realize that the rappel is more like 95 feet than the 80 feet he'd estimated, and that using an 85-foot replacement rope instead of a 110-foot rope is the cause of the problem. It means that I have to continue descending on one rope rather than two, which is less safe but doable. I have to do a series of complicated rope and hardware maneuvers to make sure I am well secured. But instead of panicking, I settle into a strange meditative calm. As Jonathan narrates the set of modifications we need to coordinate, I gracefully move through all the motions as if I've done them many times before. After making the adjustments, I finish the rappel uneventfully.

Tara's descent is equally as scrappy, but she manages without a hitch. As we bask in shady satisfaction waiting for Jonathan, she turns to me and says, "Daddy, you're so much fun to go on adventures with." It's a little moment of joy.

We complete the next big wall, another doozy, then exit the canyon through a splinterlike passageway. We have to remove our packs, walk sideways, and contract our stomachs to make the last squeeze. Once through, we de-rig, bid Jonathan adieu until next year, and walk home in the golden glow of late afternoon and post-stress relaxation.

It's our last night, so we whip up a delicious stir-fry and enjoy the serenity and isolation in glowing candlelight. Tara beats me in the card game of Spit, and we talk about the books she read in Costa Rica—John Fowles's *The Magus,* a couple of Tom Robbins novels, Edward Abbey's *The Monkey Wrench Gang* (at my urging, to ground her in the preservation battles that have helped to save canyon country). We speculate about next year. I tell her that I'd love to create a tradition of doing an annual Utah adventure—whitewater rafting, canyoneering, spring skiing, the mountain bike traverse from Telluride to Moab. She's not quite ready to sign on the dotted line, but I can see that the idea has some appeal.

"You know," she reflects, "After yesterday I couldn't imagine us trying to do this ourselves. Too scary, and I just wasn't sure I could trust myself. But after today, I feel so proud, like we really could do this ourselves.
Jonathan said the Subway has just three rappels, all with fixed anchors,
and the longest one is only thirty feet. That's totally doable."

And so we make a plan. Back to Zion next year, take the one-day
course to refresh our skills and learn jumaring in case we have to ascend
out of a tight spot, and then we're on our own. The Subway first, then
maybe Orderville. There's a world of canyons out there and an evolving
father-daughter relationship to explore.

Bow Loop and Brimstone
The Open Road, Only Better

On a Sunday morning in August 2008, I'm helping transport some chairs from a hilltop meadow above the village of Harrisville back to the Wells Memorial School in Chesham. We had borrowed them for a community supper on Friday afternoon, Eli and I and a bunch of other dads and sons loading the truck in bucket-brigade fashion. This morning, it's mostly just us dads.

I've been occupied with the logistics of efficiency and abbreviation of motion while loading the chairs, but now, driving alone along Chesham Pond, I allow the emotions of the past weekend to rise like the tide. Eli and his friend Michael aren't here because they're driving north in his old Volvo, an Old Town canoe strapped to the rack, embarking on a rite of passage for them and for me. I tear up, in a good way, in recognition of the developmental significance of the occasion.

Since the beginning of the summer—the one between Eli's freshman and sophomore college years—he and Michael have been planning this wilderness canoe trip. I was tickled when the subject first came up, Eli announcing, "I'm going to try to earn at least a couple thousand dollars this summer, but then Michael and I want to do the Bow Loop. Do you think it's okay to take a week off to do that?"

The Bow Loop is a big endeavor: a five- or six-day trip, way up near Jackman, Maine, on the Canadian border. I had managed to talk him out of going in late June, season of mists and burgeoning bugginess, convincing him that mid-August made much more sense. But I'd also tried to talk him into considering something a bit less isolated, a bit more logistically friendly. "How about the Saco, or Umbagog Lake?" But his heart was set on the Bow Loop, and there was a certain logic to it that I couldn't deny.

While Eli had spent most of the summer learning renovation—replacing floors, jackhammering rocks, reshingling roofs, reclapboarding rot, rebuilding stone walls—Tara was landscaping and waitressing on the Maine island of Vinalhaven. It was a good combination of sweat, muscle, and grit during the days and then chic refinement and polish at the only mildly classy bar and restaurant in this traditional lobstering community. But she also had the opportunity to "mess about in boats" and hop around the archipelago of islands surrounding Vinalhaven and North Haven.

I get vicarious pleasure from Eli's wilderness canoeing and Tara's islanding, but there is something more here, some momentous fulfillment of wishes. Things I've been working on with them for decades are coming together, and I want to appreciate it all fully, to grasp the fish before it slips out of my hands.

Canoeing and Islanding

Canoeing was one of the crucibles of crafting my self in my twenties. I lived for several years in southwestern New Hampshire, in a wood-heated cabin that had no running water in the winter. I had started a school, held a summer job as an edger in a two-man sawmill, traipsed the hill and marsh wilderness, and fallen in with a bunch of guys who were into whitewater canoeing. My girlfriend was in a women's group whose members had decided that they were all looking for a lumberjack who read Tolstoy—that is, a macho intellectual. I wanted to be that guy. And the challenge and finesse of whitewater contributed to the image. My whitewater pals and I honed our skills on local rivers—the Ashuelot, the Souhegan, the Millers. We worked hard to refine our strokes, work up to ever-harder rapids—the Dumplings on the West, Freight Train on the Contoocook, the tight class 4 on Otter Brook above Keene. We paddled from when the first rivers opened up, as early as late February, through the prime meltwater season of March and April, and on into the blackfly-riddled, rain-swollen runs of May.

The next step was Canada, oh Canada: the true north of the Canadian Shield. Lakes, rips, muskeg, boreal forest forever. For about a dozen winters, we huddled around woodstoves with cold Molsons in hand, planning a summer jaunt to a wilderness river. It was our raison d'etre. We pored over trip accounts, portage descriptions, and route maps. Those two weeks in the wilderness constituted the capstone experience of every summer: grueling portages, impossible rapids, four-part harmonies on polished granite under the northern lights. We'd take the ore train from Sept Îles, Quebec, heading north to Labrador, and slide the canoes down an embankment to the edge of a boggy meander 100 miles from any habitation. Or we'd strap the canoes onto the struts of a floatplane and get dropped off in a headwaters lake dotted with islets. We canoed the Moosonee, the Chamachouane, the Dumoine, the Moisie. The roar of approaching rapids and the glint of sunlight on riffles haunted my dreams. On those trips I was scared to death, overwhelmed with beauty, awestruck with expanse, more fully alive than any other time.

Starting a family put a crimp in the summer trips, but I knew I wanted to cultivate the same thirst for watery wilderness in my children. Tara's last day in utero was spent in a canoe as Wendy and I drifted the marshy backwaters of the North Branch River in Stoddard. Canoe day trips to Elephant Rock on Nubanusit Lake and the great rope swing on the island in Silver Lake were integral parts of Tara and Eli's childhood summers.

As a family, we canoe-camped an isolated lake in the Adirondacks. And as dads, my longtime canoeing buddy Toby and I took our sons on two-night canoe trips each summer when they were six to ten years old.

I remember watching Eli get blown down Loon Pond as he tried to figure out how to solo-paddle a sixteen-foot canoe one breezy afternoon—a good learning experience. Tara and I canoe-camped on a peninsula on Spoonwood Pond for a couple of nights. It was all part of my plan. I wanted our kids to be outdoorsy, paddle-savvy, comfortable in their bodies, willing to strike out on their own.

Another key set of experiences, for me and later for my family, was islanding. I think the magnetic pull of islands started to work on me during neighborhood explorations in Connecticut when I was around nine. Way back in the abandoned woods and farm fields behind my friend Kevin's house was a perfectly round pond with a perfectly round little island in the center. At the edge of the pond stood an old water tower with rickety ladders up the inside. We wanted both to climb those ladders and to make it out to that island. I made it, knees trembling, up the tower, but I wasn't sure enough about the thickness of the ice to venture out to that island the day the opportunity presented itself. Or maybe it was the lure of Wild Island in one of my favorite children's books—*My Father's Dragon* by Ruth Stiles Gannett—that provoked my island itch.

I was introduced to Maine islands in the mid-1970s when I took a Marine Ecology class with Ty Minton on Swan's Island. When I got the opportunity to teach the same course a few years later, I jumped at the chance. Combining coastal flora and fauna, fisheries economics and island sociology, my students and I created a simulation that dramatized the issue of how cormorants' theft of bait from traps affects the viability of lobstering. From that point on, I was fascinated with the culture and lifestyle of Maine's offshore communities. Continuing in the vein of waterborne exploration, my paddling partner Toby and I took advantage of the Maine Coast Trail to explore the islands between Deer Isle, Vinalhaven, and Isle au Haut via sea kayaks.

Around this same time, we initiated family vacations to these and other Maine islands—Swan's, Islesboro, Monhegan, Frenchboro. If my wilderness self was shaped on Canadian rivers, my dad self was shaped during these island summers. The kids and I swam in tidepools, climbed rocks, built fairy houses, created fantasy adventures in quarries, watched Perseid meteor showers, collected mussels, and liberated lobsters.

Our family storytelling tradition also took root and flourished here. On Swan's Island one summer, Tara composed a dramatic production based on an outdoor theatre improvisation endeavor called Adventure Game Theatre, which she had learned at summer camp and on winter weekends. A cast of princesses, monsters, heroes, and sea creatures scampered through the drizzly woods to a seaside lean-to. The willing players were her brother, the sons of a family we were vacationing with, and the various parents. The boys (emergent heroes) had to extinguish candles with their bare fingers to develop the mettle to face villains who threatened to upset the social order. Sword fights and magic spells abounded; bloodcurdling screams rent the air. All the demonic figures wound up vanquished, tossed off a rickety dock into frigid, kelp-filled brine, after which everyone huddled around a woodstove with hot chocolate and warm soup.

The intimacy of these island worlds accentuated the close-togetherness of our family experience. Being on islands meant adults and children playing and exploring together. There is something about the bounded nature of islands—that there is only just this much, no more—that makes every little thing seem valuable, more precious. This geographic and psychosocial experience of islandness was another gift I wanted to give Tara and Eli.

Kayaking around Vinalhaven with adult friends one recent summer, we stopped at Ohio Island and Raspberry Island, only a couple of acres each. Ohio was not very appealing: uninhabited and densely forested, and with the trashiest cove imaginable. Just a bit to the east, Raspberry was pristinely clean, with a charming storybook log cabin and a rampant patch of the fattest, most sumptuous red raspberries I've ever found. Just a quarter mile apart, these islands were two completely different microcosms. Could I hope that my children would appreciate such entrancing contrasts?

As parents we dream of passing along virtues to our children. We want them to be honest, forthright, independent, polite. I wanted all those dependable chestnuts, but I was also hoping to pass along certain more elusive urges and aesthetic yearnings. Canoeing was about the desire to strike out into the wilderness, to depend on your own wits and paddling skills, to sense the endless sprawl of rock and water. The lure of islands was more conceptual, perhaps best grasped from the perspective of a high place or an airplane—the awareness of a scattering of individual worlds accessible only by boat; that Darwinian sense that each island possesses a unique character, its own secret.

The Bow Loop

Eli and I, together with Michael and his father, Don, had done the Bow Loop canoe trip when Eli was just starting seventh grade. There is a harder and an easier way to do it. You can put in at Attean Lake, paddle about five miles down to the north corner, and portage over to Holeb Pond—a character-building mile-and-a-quarter carry—then paddle the length of Holeb. Here you exit into the Moose River, which swings you around in a big bow-shaped loop (hence the name) to the south end of Attean Lake. Or you can park at Attean and get a shuttle over to Holeb, skipping the big portage. Having built enough character at this point in our lives, and with two twelve-year-olds for partners, the dads chose the latter option.

The Moose is a good starter wilderness river—a few short portages, four or five manageable rapids, good campsites—but it's still wilderness. We'd figured out a way for everyone to make the trip during the first week in September, hoping for weather bliss, and we weren't disappointed. Almost frosty, full-moon nights, brisk mornings, swimmable afternoons. And the right amount of hardship. Eli and I tried a tough little rapid with an unloaded canoe one afternoon and almost wrapped the canoe around a rock. We had to pull a fishhook out of someone's finger, squirrels chewed through two of our food bags, the portage around Moose Falls was long enough to evoke shoulder pain, and the next-to-last-day paddle across Attean was into a grueling headwind, with waves breaking over the bow—one of the hardest paddles I'd experienced in a decade. The boys got a taste of the agony and the ecstasy in appropriate portions.

But now, when Eli and Michael wanted to paddle the Bow Loop by themselves, parental doubts started to kick in. For one thing, they had decided to do the whole loop, not the abbreviated version, which meant they would face that long portage on their first full day. "You've never done a canoe trip on your own. Don't you want to try something a little less complicated?" I probed. "I know you've done a good amount of whitewater kayaking, but you and Michael have never done tandem [two paddlers, one boat] whitewater canoeing. Don't you want to practice together before going off into the wilderness? Remember how we almost trashed our boat? What if you're up a stream not just without a paddle, but without a canoe? Will you be able to handle a big wind with big chop like we had that day?" And so on. I was nervous that he wasn't ready, and it was hard for me to let go.

But, in his defense, he was reasonably persuasive. "We've done this before, Dad. Michael's an Eagle Scout and he's great at all the organizing. We won't paddle any whitewater that we know is dangerous, and I really want to try this." Then the clincher: "Michael and I want to do this now so that when we're forty years old, we can take our sons on the same trip." That sealed the deal. How could I say no? Did he realize that comment would pull on my heartstrings? And of course I thought, "And maybe Gramps can come along too?"

Don and I met with them, reviewed the maps and the contents of the first aid kit, had them explain their food planning, exhorted them to remember to hang up the food bags at night, reminded them where to find the backwater turnoff to the portage trail around the falls. Neither of them had solo-portaged a canoe before (the other would be toting all the gear), but that didn't seem to faze them. They proved remarkably self-sufficient about shopping, packing, and rustling up the gear—almost too self-sufficient. I felt a bit left out.

They came to the Harrisville community supper but left early to double-bag their meals and pack the car. Then they left on Sunday morning for the six-hour drive north. That's when I found myself hijacked by strong emotions.

There are lots of different moments of maturation and separation in parenting: children learning to ride a bike, going off to that first full day of school, getting the big part in the play, leaving on a jet plane, all the different graduations. But there was something more distinctive and final about this one. This departure was self-decided and self-directed—an act of personal will. Eli was choosing to follow his own path into the wilderness, test his own mettle, and I was proud of him for so choosing. And it warmed my heart that he had chosen a path we had originally traveled together. He was following in my paddle strokes.

This was also another step in my own maturation, of having to learn who I was going to be in this post-fathering, independent-children, next stage of my life. Not being needed anymore left me with a sense of loss mixed with a sense of freedom. I was happy for Eli and a bit nervous for myself as our paths diverged.

What happened to Eli on the Bow Loop? Nothing dramatic. Just the right balance of the agony and the ecstasy, but under his own steam. The same big headwinds and big waves the first couple of days, and they muscled through it fine. There were monster thunderstorms one night, and by morning their gear was soaked, but they managed to get everything dried out at the campsite the next afternoon. He figured out how to solo-portage a canoe. (Contrary to what you might assume, it's actually easier for one person than for two to carry a canoe, but it is a skill that has to be mastered.) The camping stove malfunctioned, as they are wont to do, so they cooked over a fire most of the time. The fishing rod broke. They opted to paddle a class 3 rapid, portaged the gear, scouted the rapid for about a half hour, and then ran it. Eli paddled stern, being more experienced, and evidently did it with aplomb.

They found the fishing cabin where we had stayed six years earlier, and there was Eli's name, written in charcoal on the exterior wall, plain as day. They met hardly anyone else on the river and had that experience of pure emptiness, of being out there on their own, dependent on their own skills. Way cool.

Brimstone

Meanwhile, Tara was spending the summer between her junior and senior year of college working on Vinalhaven—her first summer not living at home. Tara's always had wanderlust. In addition to her teaching internship in Costa Rica, her young life already included a semester abroad in Chile and a summer of taking part in *commedia dell'arte* productions in French and Italian villages.

She was psychologically independent and this year was starting to grapple with the financial independence challenge, which was why she was working fifty hours a week at two jobs. For the past year I'd been consulting with the school on Vinalhaven for two or three days each month, so I had connected her with a landscape contractor. That was on top of the waitressing. A college friend of hers had a cabin they could live in rent-free. The pieces had come together.

I was tickled by her good fortune and, in truth, a bit jealous, having missed out on this kind of summer myself. Between my freshman and sophomore years, I had planned to work in Provincetown, at the tip of Cape Cod. My friend Andy and I had driven down one April weekend and landed ourselves jobs as car parkers at a seafood restaurant. I went to bed with visions of beach blanket bingo dancing in my head, until it became apparent that I needed cartilage removed from my knee. Four decades ago, this was not arthroscopic surgery. It meant I was laid up in my father's spare garret bedroom, nonambulatory, not able to go in the pool, none of my friends in town, bored out of my mind, while my friend Andy was parking BMWs, bodysurfing, and living the high life without me. The summer wasn't a total loss, though—boredom led me to read Viktor Frankl's *Man's Search for Meaning*, which made me realize that if there was going to be meaning in my life, I was responsible for carving it out. But I never did get that summer on the coast.

Tara worked hard and played hard, made lots of money and lots of friends, became an integral part of her summer island world. I rented a house on the island for a couple of weeks and it turned out to be a great way to connect with her, living closely parallel lives. I hired her to cater a dinner for about thirty people, the ending event for the school improvement project I'd been working on. She carried it off elegantly—quesadillas, gallo pinto (a Costa Rican rice and bean dish), grilled chicken with a homemade fruit salsa, and her unequaled guacamole. It was great to see her in this professional role, in charge and sure of the timing and logistics.

But what pleased me most was sensing that she was falling in love with islandness. She realized while it was happening that she was having a defining experience, the kind that shapes your aesthetics, commitments, and values. A month or so after she left the island, I got her to talk about it. Here, as recorded at the time, she describes one day during the last week of the summer that encapsulates her experience. She'd finished her jobs, her friends were leaving. . . .

Mattie was leaving, so we all meet for breakfast at Donna's place, the Surfside, the place that opens at 4:00 A.M. where all the lobstermen go. Donna's rough and tumble, looks like she works in a greasy kitchen, she's a tough girl. We are all kind of bleary-eyed so she knows to bring us big pitchers of ice water.

The weather has finally changed, the humidity is gone, there's that clear sparkly light, and we decide it's the day to go to Brimstone Island. It's that island famous for its sculptured, shiny black rocks. We disperse for an hour, meet at the ferry to see Mattie off. When the boat leaves we run out to the end of the rocks as the ferry recedes into the distance. It's the coolest departure ritual ever.

We all pile into Shane's boat, *Anna Banana*, a nice, summer people's boat, not a lobster boat. It's so different being in a motorboat on the ocean rather than a lake because of the distant horizon line, such a feeling of boundlessness. Like the open road, but even better. We power along, passing little tufts of islands, cruise around to a cove on the back side of Brimstone, weaving in through the big rocks. Then, when you get close to shore, you have to all collaborate in this fast-paced maneuver of getting all your stuff ready, jumping out, creating a fire line, and passing all the gear up to the beach. In the meantime, Shane delicately keeps the boat from getting pushed up onto the cobble by the swell.

Then we have this exquisite afternoon as lost travelers on this empty island. It has no trees, so it's just rolling, heath-y meadows of wildflowers, raspberries, and rocky, ledgy outcroppings that lead up to a high point. Remember when we hiked The Precipice on Mount Desert, early in the morning? It's like that. From the top, you waft down on gently sloping ledges. It feels like the top of the world, ripples of golden grass and flowers. No obstruction to the view. No one there but us. It feels completely timeless, like we are out of space and time. Or it feels Victorian, like in *The French Lieutenant's Woman,* and we are dressed in formal whites, lace and linens, lounging on old couches, enjoying a proper tea on the porch. Or perhaps a photo shoot.

I collect about a dozen different brimstones, each one capturing some different aspect of that day. One of them is like a map, it's mostly all black and there are bright flecks of white, which are an archipelago of islands scattered across the ocean.

Her brimstones reminded me of the polished quartz stones I had collected on an islet about fifteen miles from here a decade earlier, and which had become divination stones in the Quartz and Mica stories. Back then I was telling the story, and she was just beginning to shape the plot, by casting the stones at turning points. Now she was collecting her own stones, perhaps to become potential amulets in stories she would tell to her own children one day. The storylines were all her own. Her life had become the story she was composing.

There were other adventures that summer. A late-night, postwork jaunt over to Green's Island in duck soup fog, emerging from the mists to see a bonfire in the woods. The epic pirate party, less about grog and more about staying in character. Quarry swimming at twilight and playing on the old crane boom, a remnant of the hoisting mechanism for moving granite blocks and a great balancing challenge. The kind of summer everyone on the cusp of adulthood should have.

When I asked her the following winter in an e-mail what it meant to live on an island for the summer, Tara wrote back:

There's something that happens when you're surrounded by water. Distance feels much more significant. I mean, on land I could hypo-thetically walk to California. But, out here, I can't swim to Rockland. So just being on an island gives everyday experience a heightened sense of adventure. Everything starts on a higher level, everything is more embodied. And you realize, this is really special, a whirlwind, and it may never happen again.

  And the other element is that for many of us, it's a summer place. All of the long winter is let go of and the excitement is condensed into this little time burst. An island of time on an island at sea. The community knows itself for just a brief time, so there's a heightened vivacity and vitality. Remember that *Pirate's Plunder Treasure Book* you gave me? I brought that with me because it's such a cool book, but it also captures the romantic, otherworldly quality of islands. It's like each island has its own mythical structure.

Can you tell she had a good time? Can you tell that cold water runs in her veins and the glint of sun on waves lights her dreams? Can you imagine my inner smile as she rambled on?

I'M WRITING UP MY NOTES for this account in September, soon after these events. Last night was the autumn equinox; it's surprisingly chill for this early in the season. We're in the midst of a string of those still, crystal-line, cloudless days, like slack tide, not rising, not falling, just effortless balance. Eli and Tara are back at college; I'm back at work.

  But something changed this past summer. Eli came into his own, found his own path into the wilderness. Tara found the distinctive, mythical is-land of her unique identity. And I found that in some important way, my responsibility as a parent is done.

  There was a moment in August when, simultaneously, Eli was ne-gotiating Moose River rapids and Tara was dancing down a Brimstone meadow, "like the open road, but even better." Contemplating that moment, I know that both of my children are on paths with heart, that they walk in beauty. Now I'm just hoping to be around to teach some grandchildren to ski, to tell them stories of Quartz and Mica and the emerald chandelier, and maybe to paddle the Moose again before I canoe off to that island in the sky where, as Tara says, "everything starts on a higher level."

ACKNOWLEDGMENTS

PARENTING CHILDREN INTO NATURE is more fun when there's an extended family of parents and children playing together. My children played and explored outside with other families who shared our commitment to adventure, twilight, and following paths into mysterious woods.

Thanks to Toby, Lisa, David, and Brooks for seaweedy spring swims at Ryder Beach in Truro and for brilliant, brisk fall weekends on Lake Sunapee. Toby Wood and I learned to explore the natural world together, and we learned to parent our children into nature together. As adventure partners, we hiked the West Coast Trail on Vancouver Island, camped above tree line in the White Mountains, whitewater-canoed the wild Moisie River in Labrador and Quebec, and kayaked the Maine Island Trail. As parents, we took our children canoe-camping on New Hampshire rivers and lakes each summer, built awesome sand castles on Cape Cod beaches, and played hide-and-seek in the hidden gardens of the Hay Estate on Lake Sunapee. Toby's spirit lives on in the pages of this book and in his sons' full embrace of the natural world.

Thanks to Chris, Susan, Torin, and Cooper for rainy days on Isle au Haut and Swan's Island, where we extinguished candles with our fingers and slew evil monsters in the misty woods. Thanks to Heri, Solveig, Joschka, and Julian for rites-of-passage rituals, Thanksgiving Sardines games, and blazing bonfires. Thanks to Craig, Sarah, Anna, Marta, and Willa for visits to the Enchanted Forest and the mermaid rocks. Thanks to Jack and Peter for cozy nights at the Woodbox to prepare us for pool-hopping and gnarly skiing at Killington.

Thanks as always to my colleagues in the Education Department at Antioch University New England for their support of my writing and for their efforts to make the natural world an integral part of their parenting and teaching.

Thanks to the people of the town of Harrisville, New Hampshire, who have created a family-friendly community and have preserved the lakes, beaches, gorges, trails, hilltops, blueberries, and deep woods of our corner of the Monadnock region. Eli recently said, "I feel so privileged to have grown up in Harrisville." It's the town that many people imagine when they fantasize about the perfect place to raise a family in America.

Thanks to the many scholars and writers who have researched and advocated for the necessity of healthy relationships between children and the natural world. In particular I am indebted to Louise Chawla, Roger Hart, Richard Louv, Robin Moore, Joseph Chilton Pearce, Paul Shepard, and Nancy Wells for their keen insights and steadfast commitments.

Thanks to Jennifer Kramer who helped to conceptualize and refine many aspects of this book—from word-crafting to title-brainstorming to cover ideas to angst remediation, she's been a sounding board and constant source of inspiration.

Thanks to Diana Landau, my editor, who never gave up on the mission of this book, guided the book past publishing pitfalls, and worked tirelessly to clarify my voice in the text. Thanks to copyeditor Karen Wise for her conscientious and sensitive work. And thanks, finally, to the Sierra Club for helping to preserve this beautiful world as a place where parents and children can play, grow, and thrive.

A FEW OF THE CHAPTERS in this book originally appeared elsewhere in an earlier form. I'm grateful to the publishers for permission to recast that content here:

"A Little Bit of Love between Us and the Trees: Language and Metaphor in Tara's World" and "Moon-Jumping Nights: Reanimating the Natural World," published as the essay "A Mouthful of Flowers: Ecological and Spiritual Metaphors from Early Childhood" in *Holistic Education Review* (Brancon, VT), September 1991.

"Together in Dreamland: Bridging the Sadness of Separation," published as "Visiting Dreamland" in *Exploring the Power of Solo, Silence and Solitude*, edited by Clifford Knapp and Thomas Smith, Association for Experiential Education (Boulder, CO), 2005.

"Moving in My Heart: Divorce and Nature," published as "Moving in My Heart" in *Orion*, The Orion Society (Great Barrington, MA), September/October 2004.

"Assessing Ice: Risk and Reward on Skates," published as "Assessing Ice" in *Father Nature: Fathers as Guides to the Natural World*, edited by Paul Piper and Stan Tag, University of Iowa Press (Iowa City), 2003.

REFERENCES, FURTHER READING, AND WEBSITES

References

Arbib, Robert. *The Lord's Woods*. New York: W. W. Norton, 1971.

Bateson, Mary Catherine. *Composing a Life*. New York: Grove/Atlantic, 1989.

Britton , James. *Language and Learning*. Miami: University of Miami Press, 1971.

Chawla, Louise. "Children's Concern for the Natural Environment." *Children's Environment Quarterly 5*, no. 3 (1988).

Faber Taylor, A., F. E. Kuo, and W. C. Sullivan. "Coping with ADD: The Surprising Connection to Green Play Settings." *Environment and Behavior* 33, no. 1 (2001).

Greene, Melissa Fay. "Childhood Lost." *Parenting*, December/January 1995, 99–102.

Herter, Brooke. *Moon-Jumping*. Unpublished essay in the author's collection, 1983.

LaBerge, Stephen. *Lucid Dreaming*. Boulder, CO: Sounds True, 2004.

Louv, Richard. *Childhood's Future*. Boston: Houghton Mifflin, 1991.

———. *Last Child in the Woods: Saving Our Children from Nature-Deficit Disorder*. Chapel Hill, NC: Algonquin Books, 2005.

Seed, John, Joanna Macy, Arne Naess, and Pat Fleming. *Thinking Like a Mountain: Towards a Council of All Beings*. Philadelphia: New Society Publishers, 1988.

Shepard, Paul. "The Arc of the Mind." *Parabola* 8, no. 2 (1983).

———. *The Tender Carnivore and the Sacred Game*. Athens: University of Georgia Press, 1998.

Sobel, David. *Place-Based Education: Connecting Classrooms and Communities*. Great Barrington, MA: Orion Society, 2003.

Stafford, Kim. *A Separate Hearth: Having Everything Right*. Seattle: Sasquatch Press, 1997.

Thomas, Dylan. *Portrait of the Artist as a Young Dog*. New York: New Directions Publishing, 1940.

Werner, Heinz. *Comparative Psychology of Mental Development*. New York: International Universities Press, 1948.

Yolen, Jane. *Owl Moon*. New York: Philomel Books, 1987.

Further Reading

Cohen, David, and Stephen MacKeith. *The Development of Imagination: The Private Worlds of Childhood*. New York: Routledge, 1991.

Dillard, Annie. *An American Childhood*. New York: Harper and Row, 1987.

Eaton, Randall. *From Boys to Men of Heart: Hunting as Rite of Passage*. Santa Cruz, CA: OWLink Media, 2009.

Kiefer, Joseph. *Sharing Nature with Children*. Nevada City, CA: Dawn Publications, 1998.

Nabhan, Gary Paul, and Stephen Trimble. *The Geography of Childhood*. Boston: Beacon Press, 1994.

Pearce, Joseph Chilton. *The Magical Child*. New York: Dutton, 1977.

Sobel, David. *Beyond Ecophobia: Reclaiming the Heart in Nature Education*. Great Barrington, MA: Orion Society, 1996.

———. *Childhood and Nature: Design Principles for Educators*. Portland, ME: Stenhouse Publishing, 2009.

———. *Children's Special Places: Exploring the Role of Forts, Dens, and Bushhouses in Middle Childhood*. Tucson, AZ: Zephyr Press, 1992. Reprint, Detroit: Wayne State University Press, 2002.

Stein, Sara. *Noah's Children: Restoring the Ecology of Childhood*. New York: North Point, 2001.

Van Noy, Rick. *A Natural Sense of Wonder*. Athens: University of Georgia Press, 2008.

Young, John, Ellen Haas, and Evan McGown. *Coyote's Guide to Connecting with Nature*. Santa Cruz, CA: OWLink Media, 2008.

Websites

Building Bridges to the Outdoors
   www.sierraclub.org/youth
   This program of the Sierra Club, drawing on the organization's long experience in running wilderness outings, is committed to giving every child in America the opportunity to have an outdoor experience.

Children and Nature Network
   www.childrenandnature.org
   The "one-stop" website for all your research and networking needs on this topic, this network emerged as a vehicle for translating Richard Louv's work into practice.

Children, Youth, and Environments
www.colorado.edu/journals/cye
The best professional journal for and by academics on children and their relationship to the environment, but also valuable for parents. This is a great resource for keeping track of the leading edge of research in this field.

Connected at the Roots
http://connectedroots.wordpress.com
A beautiful and charming blog written by a Colorado mom about her explorations with her two young children. She describes exactly what I think parents and young children should be doing together outside.

EarthWalk Vermont
http://earthwalkvermont.org
One of New England's many wilderness awareness/nature mentoring programs, EarthWalk provides developmentally appropriate and thoughtful nature education for elementary school and adolescent children in central Vermont.

Free Range Kids
http://freerangekids.wordpress.com
Lenore Skenazy's website is subtitled "How to Raise Safe, Self-Reliant Children (without Going Nuts with Worry)." It contains information and insights by a parent, for parents, on how and why to encourage children to explore on their own in the city or the country.

Kids in the Valley, Adventuring!
http://kidsadventuring.org/blog
One of many family nature clubs that has emerged as part of the national children and nature movement. This one, located in the Roanoke Valley of Virginia, provides lots of good ideas for parents of elementary school children.

Kroka Expeditions

www.kroka.org

A wilderness education program in southwestern New Hampshire that integrates adventure challenge with inner spiritual growth for children. Both my children participated in excellent Kroka programs.

Let's Go Outside!

www.fws.gov/letsgooutside

A project of the U.S. Fish and Wildlife Service, this site publicizes the resources available on federal lands managed by FWS, including camping, fishing, birding, youth internships, and all manner of outdoor recreation. Separate pages are directed at kids, parents, and educators.

Natural Learning Initiative

www.naturalearning.org

The online home of Robin Moore and Nilda Cosco's design lab at North Carolina State University, one of the preeminent organizations in the country designing natural play landscapes for children at preschools, zoos, nature centers, and museums.

Nature Rocks

www.naturerocks.org

Provides an online planning tool that aims to guide families in planning nature-based activities.

Outdoor Baby

http://outdoorbaby.net

This website is for parents who want to be outdoors and active with their infants and toddlers.

Outdoors Alliance for Kids

http://sites.google.com/site/outdoorsallianceforkids

As this press release says, "OAK brings together the YMCA of the USA, REI, Sierra Club, National Wildlife Federation, Izaak Walton League of America, the Outdoor Foundation, National Recreation and Park Association, and the Children and Nature Network, collectively representing more than 30 million members, to address the growing divide between children and families and the natural world."

Wayfinder Experience
www.wayfinderexperience.com
Wayfinder is a provocative outdoors improvisational theatre experience
for adolescents. It is guaranteed to be unlike anything your teen has ever
experienced and a completely enthralling way to bond with the natural
world and with other adolescents.

Wilderness Awareness School
www.wildernessawareness.org
Located in Washington State, this is the grandparent organization
for the nature mentoring movement in North America. Jon Young's
programs and writings provide deep nature bonding experiences for
children and families across the country.

ABOUT THE AUTHOR

DAVID SOBEL is senior faculty in the Education Department of Antioch University New England in Keene, New Hampshire. He consults and speaks widely on environmental education and is the author of six previous books, including *Childhood and Nature: Design Principles for Educators* and *Beyond Ecophobia: Reclaiming the Heart in Nature Education*, acknowledged as a landmark in environmental education. He has also written many articles about children and nature that have appeared in *Orion, Encounter, Sierra, Sanctuary, Wondertime, Green Teacher,* and other publications. He has served on the editorial boards of *Encounter, Orion,* and *Community Works Journal,* for which he writes a regular column. Sobel was identified as one of the "gurus and rock stars of environmental education" in a feature article in *Teacher* magazine and as one of the 2007 Daring Dozen educational leaders by *Edutopia* magazine. He lives in Harrisville, New Hampshire, and has two grown children.